READING WITHOUT TEARS

PART SECOND

Elibron Classics
www.elibron.com

Elibron Classics series.

© 2005 Adamant Media Corporation.

ISBN 1-4021-7788-7 (paperback)
ISBN 1-4021-1962-3 (hardcover)

This Elibron Classics Replica Edition is an unabridged facsimile
of the edition published in 1897 by Longmans, Green, & Co.,
London.

READING WITHOUT TEARS.

READING WITHOUT TEARS

OR, A

Pleasant Mode of Learning to Read.

BY THE

AUTHOR OF 'PEEP OF DAY,'

&c. &c.

PART SECOND.

Forty-fourth Thousand.

LONGMANS, GREEN, & CO.

39 PATERNOSTER ROW, LONDON;

NEW YORK AND BOMBAY.

1897.

LONDON
Printed by STRANGEWAYS & SONS, Tower Street, Cambridge Circus, W.C.

HINTS TO THE TEACHER.

Learning to read is very difficult in every language, but in none more so than in English. Let the Teacher, therefore, help the Learner as much as possible.

While learning to read, the Child should call the consonants by their sounds or phonetic names, b′ d′ m′, *&c.*

The Teacher should explain the difference between these phonetic names or sounds of consonants and their common names. The Child should miss every letter not *sounded, which should be scratched out with a pencil as he comes to it. Thus in the word* lowly, *page 12 (where the mark indicates that* w *is an idle letter), the Teacher should strike it through with his pencil—*lowly. *Otherwise " idle" letters might be confused with long vowels marked —.*

The Child should name the letters in their order—unless he knows the word by sight. For instance, in reading stream, *let him say* s t r e m, *omitting the letter* a. *If he call it* strem, *let the Teacher say, "*Long *sound,* not *short, and lay a stress upon* e.*" Let the Teacher mark long vowels —, and short ones* ᴗ. *The Child will soon understand these marks. He might practise the vowels with long and short marks over them.*

Let the Teacher, with his pencil, separate initial consonants when two come together, as in sp/ell, fr/ock.

When the Child has made some progress, let him go back, as often as he wishes, to the earlier parts of the book. Let him read his favourite pages as often as he likes.

The Words in Columns in the following pages are intended, NOT *to teach Spelling, but .Reading.*

When the Child can read perfectly, these columns may be used with advantage as Spelling Lessons.

B

Twig	Street	Scrub	Sprig
tw	str	scr	spr
tw in	str ay	scr ap	spr at
tw it	str eak	scr ag	spr ain
tw ine	str eam	scr ape	spr ay
tw elve	str ide	scr eam	spr ite
tw en-ty	str ipe	skr een	
be-tw een	str ife	scra-per	

NOTE. — *Teach the Child to name every letter except the silent letters—thus, "s t r a, stray." Help the Child, if he hesitate, by pronouncing the letters quickly for him.*

A ti-ger has str ipes on his skin. Can he be made tame? Yes, he can be made tame.

A ba-by ti-ger was as fond of play as a kit-ten. It stole a bit of beef and ran a-way. But a man sei-zed it, and gave it tw en-ty str okes on its back. It did not scr eam, nor bite, but was as meek as a dog.

Rose met a str a͞y lam͞b in the lane. Rose led it home to her Mam-ma. Rose said to her Mam-ma, " May I keep it? " " No," said her Mam-ma: " we will give it back to its dam."

Pa-pa led Rose by the hand. Rose led the lamb by a str ap. Pa-pa came to a str eam. It was ea-sy for Pa-pa to str ide o-ver it. Rose step-ped on the stones in the str eam, and so got o-ver. The lamb dip-ped its feet in the str eam, as it trot-ted o-ver.

A man met Pa-pa. The man said to Pa-pa, " You have got my lamb."

Pa-pa said, " Will you sell the lamb to me ? "

" Yes,"· said the man. " You may have it for tw elve bits of sil-ver ; it is a tw in-lamb. Its mam-ma has got a sis-ter-lamb, and will not miss the str ay-lamb."

So Rose had a pet-lamb.

Ro-ses

		box	box-es
		fox	fox-es
		mix	mix-es
		fix	fix-es
rose	ro-ses	vex	vex-es
nose	no-ses	mess	mess-es
tease	tea-ses	dress	dress-es
please	plea-ses	tress	tress-es
rise	ri-ses	bless	bless-es
size	si-zes	kiss	kiss-es
seize	sei-zes	miss	miss-es
buz	buz-zes	a-muse	a-mu-ses
		sur-prise	sur-pri-ses

A fag-ot bla-zes in the grate.
Mam-ma mix-es the mess-es of oat-meal
Tw en-ty lads are at the gate.
O-pen it to let the twen-ty lads in.
Pa-pa a-mu-ses the lads by his box-es.
He sur-prises the lads by Jack-in-the-box.

Fox-es are sly and clev-er.

Fox-es are gree-dy and eat a great deal.

Fox-es hide a great deal in holes.

A fox fix-es his a-bode close to trees.

He digs a hole for his den.

He tries to get cocks and hens for his din-ner.

But if he can-not get cocks and hens, he sei-zes lin-nets and rob-ins.

If he can-not get lin-nets and rob-ins—he sei-zes rats, and toads, and moles

If a fox live by the sea—he eats crabs.

He digs up a rab-bit in his hole.

He goes to the hives to steal from the bees.

He goes to the vines to pick grapes.

Dogs try to seize fox-es.

It is not ea-sy to seize him: for he has ma-ny holes in his den, and he gets a-way by a hole.

Fox-es run a-way from a pack of dogs.

Sh eep
sh
sh y
sh ow

sh ock
sh ot
sh op
sh ip
sh in
sh ine
sh am
sh ame
sh all

sh ell
sh ed
sh ake
sh ape
sh ade
sh ut-ter
sh el-ter
sh iv-er
sh ag-gy

NOTE.—*Let the Child pronounce* s *and* h *together as one sound,* sh'. *Never pronounce in spelling any letter not sounded, but miss it. Remind the Child of long and short sounds.*

Let us play at a sh op.

You shall keep a sh op, and I will buy.

It will be a sh am sh op.

I will sell sh ells and bells, sh ips and whips, cakes and rakes, pails and nails.

I sh all buy sh ells for my grot-to.

I sh all buy a sh ip to sail in the pond.

I have a maid. Her name is Jane.

She gets up at six o'clock.

She skims the cream and makes but-ter.

She sweeps the par-lour and nur-se-ry.

She makes the beds and the cribs.

She shakes the mats and the rugs.

She bakes the cakes and the loaves.

She shells the peas and the beans.

She peels the po-ta-toes.

She fills the coal-box and the log-box.

She hems the sheets.

She cleans the knives and the sil-ver.

She o-pens the gate to vis-it-ors.

She takes up the tray at din-ner time.

She lays the plates.

She waits at din-ner.

She makes tea in the sil-ver tea-pot.

She shuts the shut-ters at sun-set.

She dress-es the babe and feeds him.

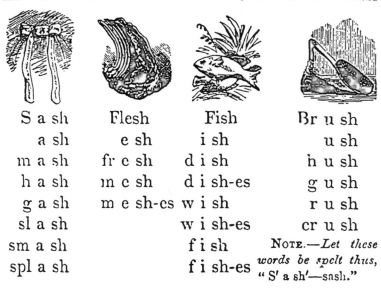

S a sh	Flesh	Fish	Br u sh
a sh	e sh	i sh	u sh
m a sh	fr e sh	d i sh	h u sh
h a sh	m e sh	d i sh-es	g u sh
g a sh	m e sh-es	w i sh	r u sh
sl a sh		w i sh-es	cr u sh
sm a sh		f i sh	
spl a sh		f i sh-es	

NOTE.—*Let these words be spelt thus,* " S' a sh'—sash."

The names of my dogs are Shock, Brush, and Dash.

Shock is shag-gy, Brush is black.

Dash is big and brave.

He likes to rush in-to the sea.

He rush-es back again, and shakes his wet coat, and spl ash-es drops o-ver me.

i sh	i sh	s h r
rub-bish	bran-d ish	shr ed
rad-ish	red-d ish	shr ill
ban-ish	pet-t ish	shr ub
rel-ish	skit-t ish	shr ug
pun-ish	slug-g ish	shr iv-el
fam-ish	bru-t ish	fish-er-man

Al-fred has a sk it-t ish po-ny.
It kicks and rush-es and runs a-way

Da-vid has a slug-g ish pony.
It will not go well.   It stops.
It stands stiil.   It wish-es to go home.
I will bran-d ish a big stick o-ver its back
to make it go on.

Ed-win has a pet-t ish pony.
It tries to go the way it likes.
It frets if it can-not do as it wish-es.

	wh eat	wh en
	wh ite	wh ip
	wh ine	wh im
	wh ile	wh im-per
Wheel	wh y	wh im-si-cal
wh	wh iff	wh is-per

NOTE.— *Teach the Child to make* w *and* h *one sound, and not to pronounce the letters separately.*

Al-fred, why do you wh ine so ?

The wh eel of my wag-on is bro-ken.

Wil-ly, why do you wh ine so ?

The lash of my wh ip is cut.

Hen-ry, why do you wh ine so ?

My white dog has got no tail.

Why do you whine and whim-per for a white dog which is not a-live ?

The tail can be nail-ed on a-gain.

A lash can be made for the whip.

The wheel of the wag-on can be mend-ed.

Fred woke on a win-ter day. He was sur-pri-sed to see snow in the gar-den.

The trees werē wh ite, the shr ubs werē white, the sh ed was white, the gate was white—ev-e-ry spot was white.

Fred wish-ed to run in the snow. He beg-ged his Mam-ma to let him run in the snow. His Mam-ma said, "Wait till the gar-den-er has made a way in the snow."

So Fred wait-ed.

His Mam-ma gave him ga-losh-es to keep his feet dry : for snow wets the feet. Fred ran in-to the sh ed to get his draȳ, and to get a spade. He dug up the snow, and fill-ed his dray. He drag-ged it to a tree, and up-set the dray. He made the snow in-to a heap. He fill-ed the dray a-gain. The heap got big-ger and big-ger.

Fred got a big box and set it on the top of the heap of snow, and he sat in it.

ack	qu ack	ake	qu ake
ell	qu ell	een	qu een
ick	qu ick	ite	qu ite

NOTE - *Teach the Child to make* q *and* u *one sound. like* kw.

Qu een

qu

qu ail	qu ick-ly	qu i-et
qu ill	qu ick-ness	qu i-et-ly
qu it	qu iv-er	qu i-et-ness

The Qu een rules o-ver the land. She is a wise and qu-iet la-dy. When you speak of her, you say, "Her Maj-es-ty;" for she is a grand la-dy. But she is low-ly. She vis-its the cots, and speaks sweet-ly to the sick. She gives a-way loaves, and beef, and flan-nel.

When she quits her home, she trav-els quick-ly by rail in a train. She has a qui-et par-lour in the train, and a so-fa to lie up-on.

Fan-ny has a tame qu ail. It is her pet. She is fond of it; for it is qui-et and clean. When the sun is set—it mur-murs sw eet-ly. It says, "Wh it, wh it, whit," in a tone like a cat's, when it purrs. It likes to eat wheat. Fan-ny goes and picks wheat for her quail. She cuts up green sal-ad, and she gets bar-ley meal for it. It flies to her when it sees her, and eats from her hand. She gives it wet sand to keep it clean.

Ann is as qui-et as a lamb. When Mamma is ill she speaks in a wh is-per, and steps as if her feet were velvet.

Jane runs qu ick-ly. When Mam-ma wish-es for her bag, Jane runs qu ick-ly to get it. Mam-ma says she is like a stag, she is so qu ick.

Lark	Stork	Turk
ar k	or k	ur k
dar k	cor k	lur k
mar k	por k	er k
par k	for k	jer k
bar k		ir k
har k		dir k

A stork is qu ite white. Wh en he stands up, he is as high as a big baby, but he is not as fat as a big ba-by. He has a slen-der neck, and a red beak, and red legs. He eats frogs, and rats, and snakes.

Did you ev-er meet a stork in the lane, or the street? No; nev-er. But storks are seen in lands o-ver the sea.

St orks are seen in Hol-land. Hol-land is o-ver the sea. It is a wet land. Storks like a wet land. Frogs like a wet land.

The men in Hol-land like the storks. No-bod-y kills the storks. No-bod-y makes the storks a-fraid.

Storks can be made quite tame. A tame stork will not peck you.

It is pret-ty to see a ba-by stroke a stork. Ba-by has a white frock and red socks, and so he is like the stork; for he is white, and he has red legs.

A lar k is not like a stork. A lar k is not big, but he can fly high.

A lark makes sweet mu-sic up in the sky. He flies so high; he seems a speck on the sky.

Por k is the fl esh of a pig.

Mut-ton is the flesh of a sh eep

Beef is the flesh of an ox.

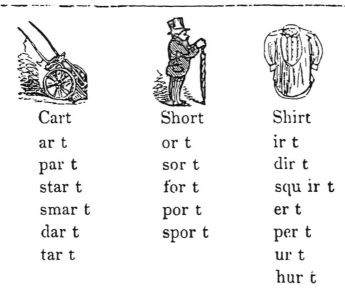

Cart	Short	Shirt
ar t	or t	ir t
par t	sor t	dir t
star t	for t	squ ir t
smar t	por t	er t
dar t	spor t	per t
tar t		ur t
		hur t

Jack drove his cart to mar-ket. He had but-ter and eggs to sell.

A man gave Jack a bit of sil-ver for a bit of but-ter.

A lad gave Jack a bit of sil-ver for six eggs.

In a sh ort time Jack had plen-ty of sil-ver in his pock-et.

A man came up to Jack, and said, "Do stop on the way." So Jack stop-ped on the way.

The man gave him port wine. Jack fill-ed a tum-bler, and fell a-sleep on the way-side. When Jack woke he got in-to his cart, and drove home. But his sil-ver was not in his pock-et. Why was Jack so sil-ly as to stop by the way? The man was a rob-ber. He rob-bed Jack while Jack was a-sleep.

When Jack got home his wife said to him, "Have you sil-ver?" "No," said Jack, "I have no sil-ver. A rob-ber has rob-bed me."

Jack was sad. His wife cri-ed. Jack said, "I will nev-er stop by the way a-gain."

Ned is a rude lad. He shot a dart at his sis-ter, and it got in-to her eye. She was sad-ly hurt. It is sport to Ned to be cru-el. He has got a squirt, and he can squirt up-on his play-fellows. He has spot-ted Tom's sh irt.

c

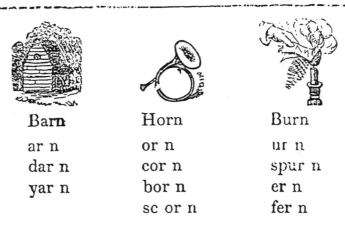

Barn	Horn	Burn
ar n	or n	ur n
dar n	cor n	spur n
yar n	bor n	er n
	sc or n	fer n

Tom was born in a wh ite cot. He was
tw elve. His sis-ter Ann was ten. He had a
Mam-ma, but he had no Pa-pa. In the dark
the cot was burn-ed up. Tom ran a-way
in time. So he was, not burn-ed up. He
drag-ged Ann by the hand, for she was a-fraid.
She scream-ed—she cri-ed. Tom's Mam-ma
hurt her legs in the flames.

    Tom said, "I will blow my horn." Men
came to help Tom's Mam-ma.

A man let Tom sl eep in his barn. Tom
had a heap of hay for his bed. He had a
sack of corn for his pil-low.

A friend let Tom's Mam-ma sl eep in a bed
in her cot. Mam-ma let Ann sl eep by her side.

A man said to Tom, "You sh all dr ive
my wag-gon. I will pay you."

So Tom had sil-ver. He got yarn for his
Mam-ma to knit socks.

She knit-ted tw en-ty red socks. She said
to Ann, "Take the socks, and sell the socks
to a la-dy. My leg is hurt. I must stay at
home; but you can go and sell."

So Ann had a bag of socks in her hand.
She knocked at a gate. The man at the gate
was rude to her. He said to Ann, "Go a-way."
A la-dy came by and said to the man, "Why
do you send her a-way?" The la-dy said to
Ann. "I will buy the socks for my ba-by"

Yard	Bird	Cord
ar d	ir d	or d
lar d	ur d	Lor d
har d	cur d	for d
car d	er d	
	her d	

A pea-cock is a big bird.   It can-not fly high like a lark, or a lin-net.

A pea-cock has a spl en-did tail.   It seems vain, as it struts and shows its fine tail.

But it has a shrill. cry.   It can-not make sweet mu-sic like a lark, or a lin-net.

Keep the pea-cock in the yard, for if it gets in-to the gar-den, it will eat up the fruit.

Will you have a fine bird, like a pea-cock?
Or will you have a sweet bird, like a lin-net?

Rose wish-ed for a sweet lin-net.

Her Mam-ma said, "Nev-er for-get to feed
the lin-net. Give it fresh seed ev-e-ry day."
Rose fed her bird for a week. But she was
ta-ken to see a la-dy, and she came home late.
The la-dy had giv-en her a box of beads.

When Rose got up in the morn, she ran to
her box, and be-gan to make a mat of blue and
white beads. She said, "Mam-ma has no mat
for the tea-pot to stand up-on, and I will try
to make her a mat." She had to go to her
les-sons. At play-time she made her mat.
But she for-got her bird. When it was dark,
she went to bed. In the morn, she did re-
mem-ber her bird. She ran to see if it was
a-live. It lay quite stiff on the sand. She
cri-ed a great deal o-ver her bird.

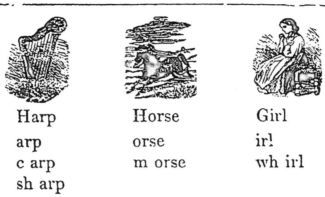

Harp   Horse   Girl
arp   orse   irl
c arp   m orse   wh irl
sh arp

El-len was a girl of six. She did not
be-have well. Her Pa-pa said, "I will take
you a drive. Jane shall go as well as you."
El-len was pleas-ed. Her nurse be-gan to
dress her. Her nurse wish-ed to wrap her in
a scar f; but El-len did not like it; so she be-gan
to scream. Pa-pa came in-to the nur-se-ry and
said, "I shall drive a-way and leave you."

But El-len did not be-lieve her Pa-pa. So
she scr eam-ed still. She ran to the win-dow
Pa-pa drove a-way. El-len cried.

urse	urze	url	arm	arve
purse	furze	curl	farm	starve
nurse		furl	harm	carve

pur-ses	farm-er	a-corn
nur-ses	re-turn	a-larm
hor-ses	de-part	for-lorn
mor-ses	tart-let	un-cork
horse-man	part-ner	un-cord
harm-less	dark-ness	bird-man
spot-less	sharp-ness	herd-man
sin-less	short-ness	Rob-ert
heed-less	pert-ness	Ru-pert
home-less	hard-ness	Al-bert
friend-less	smart-ness	Hu-bert
hope-less	rude-ness	Her-bert

Mor-ses are big and fat. Mor-ses are not
fish-es; but mor-ses live in the sea and swim well.

The

th e
th ese
th ose
th is
th at
th an
th em
th en
th ough

NOTE.- *Hitherto the Child has read* THE *without spelling. It is now time to teach him that* t h *together sound* th', *as in* "the."

Twen-ty lads and twen-ty girls will have a treat to-day. A la-dy will give them plen-ty of buns, and cakes, and jam, and but-ter, and tart-lets, and tea, for sup-per.

Then she will givē them pri-zes. The pri-zes arē for at-ten-tivē lads and at-ten-tive girls.

Al-bert, will you have this purse or that knife?

I like the knife bet-ter than the purse, for I wish to cut sticks.

Bet-sey, do you wish for this doll or for that brush?

If you please I will have the brush, for I wish to keep my tress-es neat and ti-dy.

Hu-bert, do you like this purse or that horn?

Please let me have the purse.

Then Hu-bert peep-ed in-to the purse. He said, "I see a bit of sil-ver in-side."

Da-vid, will you take these nine-pins or those hor-ses?

I like those ti-ny hor-ses bet-ter than the nine-pins, for I am fond of hor-ses.

Rob-ert shall have these nine-pins. Jan-et shall have this doll. She will like its flax-en curls. Ru-pert shall have that horn.

Clo the

b athe	w ith
ba-ther	w ith-er
br eathe	wh eth-er
l oāthe	hea-then

NOTE.—*The hard sound* th' *is used in these words*

A farm-er came to his gate. A lad was close to the gate with a pack-et in his hand.

The farm-er said, "Why do you stand in my yard? Do you wish to speak to me?"

The lad said, "I have run a-way from my home. I have not a mor-sel to eat."

The farm-er said, "Why did you run a-way?"

The lad said, "A cru-el man beat me. I had no friends to take my part. So I ran a-way. My clo the s arē in this packet."

The farm-er said, "Have you no Pa-pa nor Mam-ma?"

"No," said the lad.

The farm-er had pit-y on the lad, and bade him en-ter his a-bode. He gave him sup-per and a bed.

When the lad rose from his bed, the farm-er bade him bathe in a big tub. Then he led the lad in-to the yard, and bade him fill the cart with stones. The lad did as he was bid.

So the farm-er was pleas-ed, and he said to the lad, "I will clothe you, and feed you."

When he was at home the farm-er said to the lad, "God made you, and keeps you a-live. He for-gives sins. He bids you not tell lies, nor steal."

The lad cried, and said, "I am bad. I did tell lies. I stole the pack-et. I ran a-way from my friends." The farm-er said. "Go home, and beg to be for-giv-en."

Th ief

th in	th ump	th un-der
th ick	th irst	th ir-ty
th orn	th irs-ty	th ir-teen
th umb̄	th ick-et	Th urs-day

NOTE.—*The Teacher can now point out the difference between the* hard *sound of* th' *as in* "the," *and the* soft *sound as in* "thief."

A thief steals. It is wick-ed to steal. God has bid us not to steal.

A thief met a man. He slip-ped his hand in-to his pock-et. He seiz-ed the man's purse. The man did not see the thief take his purse. When he came home he miss-ed it. He said. "A thief has ta-ken it. I can-not buy meat this week. I can-not buy a coat, though this coat is rag-ged. I can-not buy a hat, though this hat has a hole in it. I have no sil-ver to buy with. The thief was cru-el to steal my purse."

Kate pick-ed a rose for Mam-ma.

A thorn ran in-to her thumb.

Kate feels pain. She can-not use her hand. Pa-pa wish-es to see her thumb.

Show it to Pa-pa.

Can Pa-pa take a-way the thorn? Yes.

Will Kate stand still while Pa-pa tries to take a-way the thorn? Pa-pa will not hurt you, my sweet Kate.

Kate did not cry. Her hand did not shake She did not feel pain. Her thumb is well.

When it thun-ders, it seems as if God spoke. Thun-der makes us a-fraid. But God can keep us from harm. Let us pray to Him when we are a-fraid. Then we need not be a-fraid of thun-der, nor of li-ons, nor of dark-ness, nor of the sea, when the waves dash on the rocks.

thr   thr

thr oat   thr ush

thr ow   thr ash

thr ee   thr ive

Thr one   thr ill   thr o u gh

The Queen sits on the throne of this land.

Sal-ly was thr ee.   Yet she was a thief.
Nurse came in-to the nur-se-ry. She had a
plate in her hand with thr ee pats of but-ter.
The plate was so low that Sal-ly got her hand
in-to it and seized a pat of but-ter.   She
ran into the back-nur-se-ry to eat the pat.
Nurse ran to her, and made her give up the
but-ter.   Nurse said that Sal-ly was a thief.
Sally was a-sha-med.   She did not wish to
steal a-gain.

Pa-pa said to Wil-ly, "**Do** not thr ow stones."

But Wil-ly did thr ow **thr** ee stones, and so
he broke the win=dow-pane.

Mar-tin came to see his Grand-pa-pa.

He came in the train.   His nurse sat by him. It was dark when he stop-ped at the gate, and he was ta-ken up to bed.

When he a-woke he got up, and be-gan to play.   He ran in-to the yard.   A lad-der was in the yard.   Mar-tin wish-ed to get up the lad-der. A lad said to him, " Do not get on the lad-der." But Mar-tin said, " I will.   He tri-ed to get up to the top.   But the lad-der fell back, and Mar-tin fell back and broke his arm.   He was in pain.   He cried.   The nurse ran in-to the yard.   She pick-ed him up.   She got in-to a cart.   Mar-tin sat on her knee.   A man drove Mar-tin to see the doc-tor.   The doc-tor tied a band on his arm.

Mar-tin came back pale and sad.   Grand-pa-pa said, "You had bet-ter go home; for if you stay in my farm, you may get in-to harm."

truth	faith	E-dith
Ruth	saith	Ju-dith
heath	birth	Ber-tha
teeth	mirth	Eth-el
		Cath-a-rine
Seth	Mar-tha	Tim-o-thy
Heth	Ar-thur	E-lis-a-beth

Yōuth
uth

NOTE.—*The Teacher will point out that these words have the* SOFT *sound of* th', *and not the hard sound as in* "with."

Speak the truth. Be not a-fraid to con-fess a mis-take or a sin.

Mar-tha speaks the truth. The rule was to shut the gate, and so to keep the sheep from the gar-den. But Mar-tha for-got to shut the gate, and thir-ty sheep got in and be-gan to eat the peas, and the beans, and the greens

Mar-tha was not a-fraid to speak the truth. She said, "I for-got to shut the gate. Pray for-give me. I will try nev-er to for-get a-gain."

see-eth   *means the same as*   sees

he see-eth   ,,   he sees

she eat-eth   ,,   she eats

it feed-eth   ,,   it feeds

he speak-eth   [*Let the Teacher*   he speaks

he ma-keth   *tell the Child that*   he makes
           see-eth means the

he ha-teth   *same as sees.*]   he hates

he dwell-eth   ,,   he dwells

she giv-eth   ,,   she gives

she seek-eth   ,,   she seeks

God see-eth men from His throne in the sky. He giv-eth us din-ner day by day. He ma-keth corn to grow for us to make in-to loaves. He ma-keth the rain to wet the land. He ma-keth the sun to ri-pen the corn. He feed-eth the li-ons and the ra-vens, and the sheep and the rob-ins.

He sleep-eth not. When we sleep in the dark, He is still a-wake,

Veil

ey ei

pr ey	r ein	n eigh
th ey	sk ein	neigh-bour
wh ey	o-b ey	ei gh t
v ein	dis-o-bey	w eight

NOTE.—*Tell the Child that* ey *and* ei *sound like* a; *and let him call them* a *when he spells a word*

Ber-tha has a hive of bees. She feeds them with sweet stuff. She ties a veil o-ver her bon-net while she feeds them. She is a-fraid of her bees. They will not o-bey her.

Seth feeds the hor-ses. They are glad to see him. They gal-lop to meet him. When Seth leaves them, they neigh.

Mam-ma gave E-dith a play-shop on her birth-day. It was fill-ed with jars of tea, and co-coa, and rai-sins. E-dith can weigh the tea in scales, and sell it to her doll.

The li-on drags his prey in-to his den. He can drag a sheep, though it is a great weight.

O-bey Mam-ma when you are from home.

El-len did o-bey her Mam-ma, when she was a-way from home. El-len was weak and sick-ly, and her Mam-ma did not let her eat muf-fins, or plum-buns, or plum-cake. A neigh-bour wish-ed El-len to take tea with her. El-len's Mam-ma let her go. But she beg-ged El-len to o-bey her rules when she was at tea.

El-len got on her po-ny, and Ruth led her by the rein. El-len stop-ped at her neigh-bour's gate. She was shown in-to the par-lour. Eight girls came to play with El-len. They had plum-cake, and plum-buns, and muf-fins. But El-len re-fu-sed to take a ti-ny bit. She did o-bey her Mam-ma. A girl gave her a cup of whey. El-len did not re-fuse the whey; for her Mam-ma had not for-bid-den her to take whey.

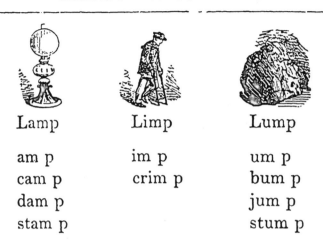

Lamp	Limp	Lump
am p	im p	um p
cam p	crim p	bum p
dam p		jum p
stam p		stum p

A cam-el has a hump on his back. He was born with it.

Bob has a bump on his nose. He hit his nose in the dark, and the bump came.

Jane has a lump in her thr oat. She was in the damp in the dark, and she got a lump in her throāt.

James can jump o-ver a high stile; but John is lame, and he limps as he goes.

We have a pond in the gar-den. Pa-pa will take us on Fri-day to bathe in the pond. We must not bathe a-lone. Rob-ert fell in-to the pond. Tray was close by. He jump-ed in-to the pond, and drag-ged him to the land. Rob-ert is so fond of Tray. He says that Tray sa-ved his life; and so he did. Rob-ert was three when he fell in.

A ti-ger is cru-el. He eats men; but men kill ti-gers when they can.

A ti-ger seiz-ed a man. The man lay un-der the ti-ger. The man was a-fraid. He had a dirk in his shirt. He stuck the dirk in the ti-ger's bod-y. The ti-ger di-ed. The man was not hurt.

The man got the skin of the ti-ger. It is fine and grand. It has str ipes on it. It will do as a rug for the feet, or a cl oak for the back.

Nest	Fist	Dust
est	ist	ust
best	list	must
west	mist	crust
jest	as-sist	trust
fat	fat-ter	fat-test
big	big-ger	big-gest
hot	hot-ter	hot-test
thin	thin-ner	thin-nest
wet	wet-ter	wet-test
short	short-er	short-est
clean	clean-er	clean-est
quick	quick-er	quick-est
slow	slow-er	slow-est
wise	wi-ser	wi-sest
hap-py	hap-pi-er	hap-pi-est

Min-nie had a rope to skip with. She ran quick-ly up the gar-den and back a-gain, and she skip-ped as she went. Grand-pa-pa was at the win-dow, and he said that Min-nie was the best skip-per he had e-ver seen. " But do not be vain," he said, " for God made you so quick, and God can make you the weak-est of girls. I will take you to see a girl weak-er than a babe." So Grand-pa-pa led Min-nie to see the weak girl. She was in bed. She seem-ed to be the thin-nest of girls. But she said, "I am the hap-pi-est of girls, for I feel God is with me."

Hen-ry str uck Rose with his fist. Pa-pa ti-ed up his wrists with a bit of list. Hen-ry stamp-ed with his feet when his wrists were ti-ed. Pa-pa said, "When you are qu i-et I will un-tie the list." So Hen-ry was qui-et, and his wrists were un-ti-ed.

	eft	emp	con-tent
	left	hemp	ab-sent
	cleft	esk	pres-ent
		desk	mo-ment
Tent	elt	ext	tor-ment
ent	belt	next	hon-est
sent	melt		in-sect
pent	smelt	ept	per-fect
spent	knelt	kept	ex-pense
rent	felt	slept	im-mense
lent		wept	de-fend
bent	elm	ense	a-mend
went	helm	sense	re-qu est

Rob-ert and Al-bert wcrē fond of play. On Sa-tur-day they had time to play.

Rob-ert said, " Let us go and fly the kite." "Yes," said Al-bert, " we will go. It will a-muse me to fly the kite. But let us go

first and take a fag-ot to Nan-ny " " No,"
said Rob-ert; " I do not wish to take her a
fag-ot. Pa-pa did not tell me to take it."
" But," said Al-bert, " Pa-pa wish-es us to
take it." " Pa-pa is ab-sent," said Rob-ert.
" He will not know wh eth-er we havē ta-ken
it or not." Al-bert said, " I will o-bey Pa-pa
when he is ab-sent the same as when he is
pres-ent." " But I will do as I like best,"
said Rob-ert. So he went a-way with his
kite.

Al-bert went and cut sticks, and tied
them up with a rope, and so made a fag-ot.
He ran quick-ly to Nan-ny's cot, and made
her hap-py with this pres-ent. Then he ran
to fly the kite with Rob-ert. He felt hap-py;
but Rob-ert felt tor-ment in his heart. Though
the kite went up an im-mense way, his heart
was sad. for he had dis-o-bey-ed Pa-pa.

	ild	ift	asp
	gild	lift	hasp
	būild	gift	rasp
		swift	
Milk	ilt		ant
ilk	hilt	uft	pant
silk	tilt	tuft	
	qu ilt		ast
int	spilt	unt	hast
lint		hunt	
print	isk		print-er
	brisk	ulk	hunt-er
ilm	wh isk	skulk	build-er
film	risk	bulk	pan-ther

A dog na-med Jump-er goes to buy milk at a milk-shop. When his mis-tress wish-es for milk, she gets a tin can, and drops a pen-ny in-to it. The clev-er dog takes up the can be-tween his teeth, and runs to the milk-shop. Then he knocks at the gate, or else he barks, till the gate is o-pen-ed. When the milk-man o-pens the gate, he takes the pen-ny and he gives the dog milk in the can. The dog runs sw ift-ly home. He nev-er stops to play with dogs by the way, nor to hunt cats, nor to steal meat, nor to pick bones. When he gets home, his mis-tress sees that he has not spilt a drop of milk.

A dog na-med Ro-ver is a beg-gar. When he sees a well-dress-ed man in the streets he jumps up-on him, and feels the pock-ets of his coat He means to say, "Give me a pen-ny." If the man un-der-stands the dog, he gives him a pen-ny. This pen-ny the dog takes be-tween his teeth, and goes to a baker's shop close at hand, to buy a cake. He gives the pen-ny to the ba-ker, and then takes up cake and runs home to eat it.

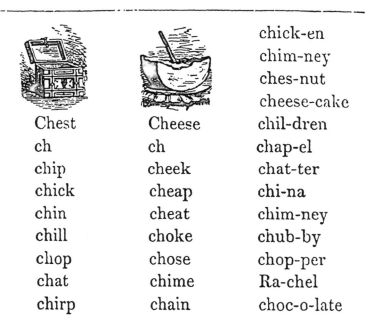

		chick-en
		chim-ney
		ches-nut
		cheese-cake
Chest	Cheese	chil-dren
ch	ch	chap-el
chip	cheek	chat-ter
chick	cheap	chi-na
chin	cheat	chim-ney
chill	choke	chub-by
chop	chose	chop-per
chat	chime	Ra-chel
chirp	chain	choc-o-late

Ra-chel and Char-ley were left a-lone
at home. Ra-chel was in the par-lour
knit-ting when Char-ley rush-ed in and said,
" I wish for my din-ner."   Ra-chel said, " I
will cut you a bit of cheese to eat with a

crust, if you need it: but I think you had bet-ter wait for din-ner." "Oh, I do not wish for cheese," said Char-ley. "Let me havē a cheese-cake from the pan-try." "But," said Ra-chel, "we shall be seen, if we go in-to the pan-try, for Wid-ow Chase sits at her win-dow, and can see in-to the pan-try." "Oh, then, let me have a bit of the chick-en in the lar-der," said Char-ley. "Oh," said Ra-chel, "the ba-ker will go by with his low cart, and he may see us in the lar-der." "Then," said Char-ley, "can you not pick ches-nuts from the tree and roast them?" "Oh," said Ra-chel, "the man is dig-ging close by." "Oh, then, can-not you get a stick of choc-o-late from the dark clos-et? We can-not be seen in the dark." "Oh, stop, stop," said Ra-chel, "the Lord can see in the dark." Char-ley's chub-by cheeks were red with shame.

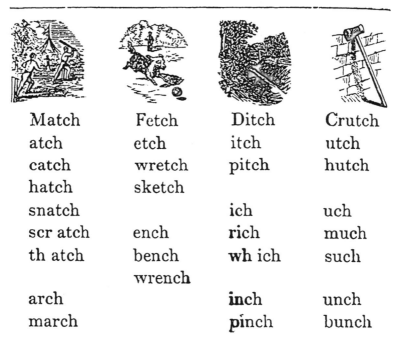

Match	Fetch	Ditch	Crutch
atch	etch	itch	utch
catch	wretch	pitch	hutch
hatch	sketch		
snatch		ich	uch
scr atch	ench	rich	much
th atch	bench	wh ich	such
	wrench		
arch		inch	unch
march		pinch	bunch

Snap-per was a wise dog. He had a black
coat and yel-low feet. He ran quick-ly. He
bark-ed well. He li-ked much to catch rats,
and to kill them. Rats ran quick-ly in-to
holes when Snap-per went by. They hid

them-selves; but Snap-per smell-ed them, and tri-ed to catch them.

But Snap-per was not cru-el, as you shall see.

Three chil-dren kept rab-bits in a hutch in the yard. The hutch was high up. A hole was in the hutch un-der a bed of hay. Three ba-by rab-bits lay on that bed of hay. The hay kept the ba-by rab-bits safe. But a man came to clean the hutch. The bed of hay was ta-ken a-way. Then the ba-by rab-bits fell through the hole up-on the grav-el be-low. The man did not see them drop.

Snap-per went to the wee rab-bits. Did he eat them? No. He lift-ed up a ba-by rab-bit with his teeth, and ran with it in-to the kit-chen, and laid it on the rug. So he did to the three rab-bits. The chil-dren were pleas-ed. They pat-ted Snap-per, and prais-ed him, and said he was the best and wis-est of dogs.

teach-er
preach-er
pitch-er
ditch-er
arch-er

Peach

each

reach

beach

teach

scr eech

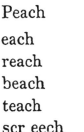

Coach

oach

poach

poach-er

ap-proach

satch-el
church-yard
match-box
Rich-ard
lunch-ēon

Jack was a fine big dog. He was brave
and live-ly. His home was by the sea. He
spent much of his time on the beach. He
liked to leap o-ver the big stones, scam-per
up the cliffs, or rush in-to the sea to fetch a
stick. The sail-ors were fond of him, and
gave him bits of meat as well as bones. He
was nev-er chain-ed up in a ken-nel. He

did as he li-ked.   He was a clev-er dog, but
he was rude and self-ish.

If he met a dog in the street, or on the
beach, he seiz-ed him with his teeth, and
nev-er let him go till he had sha-ken him.
So no dog li-ked to ap-proach him.

As he lay a-sleep on the road a coach ran
o-ver him and crush-ed him, but did not kill
him.   A doc-tor tri-ed to make him well.

When he got well—he went a-gain in the
street, and on the beach; but he was not
rude as he u-sed to be.   He nev-er ill-treat-ed
a dog a-gain, and he went to church on Sun-
days.   Why did he go to church?   I can-not
tell.   Dogs need not go to church, for they
can-not pray to God: but Jack chose to go.
He came in time, and sat quite still.   He sat
in the best seat in the church.   He stay-ed till
the end.   Then he went home qui-et-ly.

E

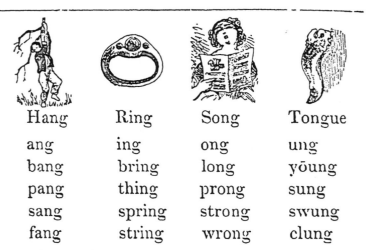

Hang	Ring	Song	Tongue
ang	ing	ong	ung
bang	bring	long	yŏung
pang	thing	prong	sung
sang	spring	strong	swung
fang	string	wrong	clung

When I came home my twelve chil-dren were in the par-lour.

Mar-tha was nurs-ing the in-fant.

Ber-tha was sing-ing a song.

Ed-ward was writ-ing a let-ter.

E-li-za was mak-ing a frock.

Jane was knit-ting a stock-ing.

Ar-thur was spin-ning a hum-ming top

Edith was skip-ping with a rope.

Rich-ard was rid-ing on a rock-ing horse.

Em-ma was set-ting her tea-things.

Ger-trude was dress-ing her doll.

Rob-ert was play-ing with his cart.

Chil-dren, let us go in-to the gar-den.

I will sit under this tree while you are run-ning and jump-ing and swing-ing.

Let us go to see the hives of bees.

Do not ap-proach too close to the hive, the bees may sting you. They have sharp stings. Rob-ert goes close to the hive, and cries, " A bee, a bee has stung my knee."

Brush a-way the bee from Rob-ert's knee.

The bee has stung his fat and rud-dy knee.

Ed-ward, take a-way the sting.

E-li-za, fetch a blue-bag from the kit-chen.

Rub the blue-bag on Rob-ert's knee.

Bring play-things to a-muse Rob-ert.

It was wrong of Rob-ert to dis-o-bey.

Bank	Drink	Sunk
ank	ink	unk
thank	think	trunk
prank	chink	monk
blank-et	trink-et	monk-ey

Kate went a long way with her Pa-pa. She rode on a don-key, and her Pa-pa went a-long by her side. When din-ner time came, Kate made the don-key stop. She sat up-on a bank, while the don-key was graz-ing close by. The don-key was thirs-ty, and he went to a stream to drink.

NOTE.—*Let the Teacher point out the sound of* ang, ing, ong, ung, *in the above words.*

Then Pa-pa laid the din-ner on the green bank. He gave Kate a bit of his loaf and of his cheese, and a leg of a chick-en, and a peach. When they had di-ned, they went on.

As the sun was set-ting they came to an inn. They drank tea at the inn. Kate got ink and pa-per, and wrote a let-ter to her mam-ma. Kate slept in a bed with clean white cur-tains.

When it was day a lad led the don-key to the stone steps of the inn, and Kate got on, and Pa-pa went by her side. They went a long way that day. They li-ked to see sheep feed-ing on the hills, and chil-dren play-ing on the green.

In three days Pa-pa said, " Let us go home, or Mam-ma will be think-ing we shall nev-er re-turn."

Mam-ma was sit-ting at the win-dow with the ba-by when Pa-pa and Kate stop-ped at the gate. She ran to meet them.

too	food	roof	booth
soon	brood	hoof	smooth
spoon	room	coop	roost
fool	groom	hoop	choose
pool	broom	stoop	tooth
cool	goose	poor	bal-loon
school	loose	moor	saloon

Moon

oo

You can-not reach so high as the moon. No bird can fly up to the moon. No-bod-y can see the things in the moon. A bal-loon can-not go up to the moon.

A goose is a fool-ish bird. It hiss-es at the chil-dren when they ap-proach it. "Fool-ish Mis-tress Goose, we wish to see the young brood that fol-low you. You have such pret-ty yel-low gos-lings." But the goose went on his-sing. The chil-dren ran a-long the moor. They soon got to school.

As they came back from school, they spoke to the goose again.

" Thank you, Mis-tress Goose; we have been wri-ting with a quill from a goose's wing; so we shall grow wise, though you are fool-ish." The poor goose turn-ed a-way with her brood, and soon was seen swim-ming in the pool.

A duck is not so big as a goose. She nev-er hiss-es, but she says "Quack" in an ug-ly tone.

She leaves her young brood too much, and ma-ny of her duck-lings die. A hen is a bet-ter nurse. So a duck's eggs were given to a hen. The hen led the duck-lings on the green and on the moor. When the duck-lings came to a pond, they ran in, and be-gan to swim. The poor hen flap-ped her wings and scream-ed; for she was a-fraid.

Note.—*All these words have the sound of oo, though not spelt with oo*

oo	oo	oo
do	who	tomb
to	whom	soup
two	whose	lose

Shoe

oo

Who are those two rag-ged chil-dren? They are the chil-dren of a man, who lies in the church-yard.

Poor chil-dren! Who feeds them?

They have no food.

Who clothes them? They have no clothes.

Who teach-es them? They have no teach-er.

We will give them soup and a loaf.

Give each of them a spoon and a plate.

The soup will get cool while the loaf is cut-ting up. The chil-dren shall go to school. The shoe-ma-ker shall make them shoes and boots.

Ann had a hen and a brood of chick-ens She kept them under a coop in the gar-den. She had ten chick-ens at first. But soon she be-gan to lose her chick-ens.

The cat came and seiz-ed two chick-ens.

Two chick-ens died from eat-ing too much hard food.

Two were crush-ed un-der the coop.

Two chick-ens fell in-to the pool.

Two chick-ens werē trod-den up-on by the horse's hoofs.

Then Ann had no chick-ens left.

Why can-not Het-ty eat her food this morn-ing? She has eat-en sweet things. Bob went to the shop to buy tarts and sweet drops, and he gave them to Het-ty, and so she is quite ill, and can-not eat plain food. Het-ty can-not go to school to-day. She can-not play with her hoop to-day. She must be shut up in her bed-room.

 God made the land and sea, the sun and moon and stars, the birds, and beasts and fish-es.

God made Ad-am's bod-y of the dust. Then God breath-ed on him, and so Ad-am had a soul.

God gave Ad-am a wife. Her name was Eve.

God let them live in a sweet gar-den.

God gave Ad-am the fruit of the trees for his food. But He said, " Do not eat of the tree in the midst of the gar-den. If you eat of it, you shall die."

Did Ad-am and Eve o-bey God ? At first they did. But Sa-tan, the wick-ed dev-il, came to tempt them to dis-o-bey. He was like a ser-pent when he spoke to Eve.

He said, " You shall not die, but you shall be made wise like God." So fool-ish Eve ate, and gave the fruit to Ad-am.

When Ad-am had eat-en the fruit he was a sin-ner. He had dis-o-bey-ed God

To dis-o-bey God is sin.

Ad-am and Eve were sin-ners.

Ad-am did not wish to see God.

So he hid him-self un-der the trees.

Did the trees hide Ad-am from God?

O no. God did see Adam, for God can see ev-e-ry bod-y.

God spoke to Ad-am and to Eve.

He said, "You are dust, and you shall be dust a-gain." Ad-am's bod-y was made of dust.

When a per-son dies, his bod-y turns to dust.

God did not let Ad-am and Eve stay in the sweet gar-den of E-den.

Why not? They were sin ners. Sin-ners must not stay in the gar-den of God.

God sent Je-sus to die for sin-ners, and to save them from sin. Je-sus was nail-ed to a tree.

NOTE.—*Let the Child pronounce a w as one sound.*

Claw

aw au

jaw	law	awl	lawn
paw	saw	crawl	fawn
caw	gnaw	Paul	yawn
daw	draw	sprawl	hawk
maw	straw	bawl	Maud
paw	thaw	shawl	Claude

When Pa-pa came home he said to Maud, "I have got a big bird with me." Maud wish-ed to see it, for she was fond of birds.

But when she saw this bird, she did not like it. The bird was a hawk. He had sharp claws, and he had a sharp bill.

Maud saw the hawk eat his din-ner. Raw flesh was his food. Maud did not like the red meat. Pa-pa let the hawk live in the gar-den to keep a-way birds from the fruit. Maud was a-fraid to go in-to the gar-den.

Maud was play-ing with her doll in a cor-ner of the nur-se-ry. Paul was a ba-by sit-ting on his nurse's knee. He saw Maud in the cor-ner with her play-things, and he wished to get to her.

Maud had made a tent with a shawl, and she had laid her doll to sleep on a low stool, when Paul crawl-ed up to her, and seiz-ed the doll. As soon as he got it, he be-gan to gnaw it. Maud snatch-ed it from him, and gave him a hard slap. Paul be-gan to bawl. Nurse ran to help him.

"Oh, Miss Maud!" she said, "why did you treat him so ill?" Maud re-pli-ed, "He mauls my things with his young paws." "O why do you speak so of the dar-ling ba-by?"

Next day Maud gave Paul a doll. It was a red bag stuff-ed with straw, and wrap-ped up in a yell-ow shawl.

taught	fault	saw-yer
caught	haunt	Au-tumn
naugh-ty	jaunt	Au-gust
haugh-ty	cause	gau-dy
daugh-ter	be-cause	taw-dry
slaugh-ter	Lau-ra	awk-ward

The cat has scratch-ing paws.
The dog has bit-ing jaws.
The hawk has cru-el claws.
The crow flies high and caws.
The rat has teeth and gnaws.
Clau-di-us ham-mers, chops, and saws.
In spring the birds be-gin to sing.
In sum-mer the corn is reap-ed.
In au-tumn the grapes are ripe.
In win-ter snow whi-tens the land.

Did you ev-er see a crab? A crab has long claws, and it can pinch hard with its claws. It lives in the sea.

The fish-er-men have caught plen-ty of crabs. Pa-pa wish-es to buy a crab. He buys it, and lets it lie in a bas-ket. Claude wish-es to see the crab. He is just go-ing to tōuch it. Pa-pa says, "Do not touch it." But Claude re-plies, "Why not?" "It will hurt you," says Pa-pa. "No, it will not," re-plies Claude. He touch-es it. He screams, he bawls, he bel-lows. The crab has caught his thumb in its claws, and it will not let go. Pa-pa sei-zes the crab, and makes it o-pen its claws. Claude goes on bawl-ing, for he is still in pain. It was naugh-ty of him to dis-o-bey. Nurse wraps up his thumb in wet rag. Soon it is well. Claude begs Pa-pa to for-give his fault. He says, "I will o-bey next time,"

NOTE. — *Let the Teacher explain that the last syllable in these words is not long as* blee, *but short as* bl´.

Ta-ble ble   Cra-dle dle

a-ble	buh-ble	la-dle	hud-dle
ca-ble	am-ble	nee-dle	pud-dle
sta-ble	ram-ble	bea-dle	mud-dle
fa-ble	scram-ble	i-dle	can-dle
fee-ble	bram-ble	bri-dle	han-dle
Bi-ble	trem-ble	sad-dle	dan-dle
bab-ble	thim-ble	pad-dle	spin-dle
dab-ble	jum-ble	med-dle	kin-dle
peb-ble	mum-ble	fid-dle	swin-dle
nib-ble	crum-ble	mid-dle	fon-dle
scrib-ble	grum-ble	rid-dle	bun-dle
hob-ble	mar-ble	cod-dle	cur-dle
cob-ble	bau-ble	cau-dle	hur-dle

The fam-i-ly at the farm are nev-er i-dle. They get up soon in the morn-ing. In win-ter they have can-dles or lamps to get up by.

The farm-er has sev-en daugh-ters.

The farm-er and his wife give them or-ders.

Su-san, take a nee-dle and thim-ble, and darn the stock-ings.

Ra-chel, take a sad-dle and bri-dle, and go on the don-key to mar-ket, and sell the but-ter and eggs, and cheese and cream.

Ruth, take a la-dle, and fill the cans with soup for the poor peo-ple.

Han-nah, take up ba-by from his cra-dle, and dan-dle and fon-dle him till tea-time.

Bet-sey, take the chil-dren a ram-ble, and let them scram-ble a-mong the hills.

Kate, go and feed the fee-ble lamb with milk in the sta-ble.

Jane, read the Bi-ble to the blind shep-herd.

Ket-tle	Ap-ple	Ea-gle
tle	ple	gle
set-tle	tip-ple	bea-gle
net-tle	crip-ple	o-gle
cat-tle	sup-ple	bu-gle
rat-tle	am-ple	
bat-tle	tram-ple	strag-gle
prat-tle	sam-ple	hag-gle
lit-tle	tem-ple	wrig-gle
whit-tle	sim-ple	bog-gle
bot-tle	dim-ple	smug-gle
pot-tle	pim-ple	strug-gle
scut-tle	rum-ple	
man-tle	crum-ple	gar-gle
star-tle	pur-ple	gur-gle
tur-tle	peo-ple	

Kit-ty had a set of lit-tle tea-things. Her Mam-ma gave her a great treat. She let her in-vite her lit-tle friends to tea. They came at five o'clock. Kit-ty help-ed to un-tie the man-tles of her lit-tle friends. She did not rum-ple nor crum-ple them; but laid them neat-ly on the bed.

She had a ket-tle to make tea with. She had a plate of ap-ples on the ta-ble. The girls had much prat-tle to-geth-er at tea.

When tea was o-ver they went to see the ea-gle in the gar-den. It made them trem-ble to see his strong claws and sharp beak.

Kit-ty led them next to see her rab-bits nib-ble tur-nips. Her young friends did not med-dle with the fruit in the gar-den, nor did they tram-ple on the beds. As they came home they were stung by the net-tles, but they did not grum-ble.

Buc-kle	Muz-zle	Ruf-fle
kle	zle	fle
knuc-kle	puz-zle	muf-fle
cac-kle		shuf-fle
tac-kle	daz-zle	snuf-fle
spec-kle		scuf-fle
frec-kle	miz-zle	truf-fle
sic-kle	driz-zle	
fic-kle	friz-zle	snaf-fle
pic-kle	griz-zle	baf-fle
pric-kle		
tric-kle		tri-fle
coc-kle		sti-fle
trea-cle		
spar-kle		

El-len was a fic-kle lit-tle girl. Her Mam-ma let her do as she pleas-ed on her birth-day. El-len wish-ed to go to the hills and dine.

She fill-ed a big box with things for din-ner. When she got to the spot, she be-gan to cry. I do not like this spot," she said; "The sun daz-zles my eyes. I am a-fraid frec-kles will make my nose ug-ly." Then she o-pen-ed the box. She did not like the beef and the pie. She said, "I wish for a bot-tle of pic-kles, and for a bot-tle of trea-cle, and for a dish of coc-kles." Then she be-gan to grum-ble. Soon she play-ed with her sis-ters. Then she scream-ed, be-cause the bram-bles, and the net-tles, and the pric-kles, hurt her. Then it be-gan to miz-zle and to driz-zle. Her Mam-ma muf-fled her up in her shawl, and El-len said, "You sti-fle me."

Cow
ow

NOTE.—*Let the Child be taught that* ow *and* ou *are generally sounded, as in these words.*

ow	out	owl
ou	pout	fowl
now	spout	howl
how	trout	growl
sow	stout	scowl
vow	snout	
bow	shout	town
brow	a-bout	drown
Thou		crown
plough	loud	frown
bough	proud	brown
	crowd	
mouth	cloud	pouch
south	shroud	crouch

In a land far a-way a shep-herd had a flock. In the day-time he led his flock to feed on the green hills, and to drink from the run-ning streams.

When it was dark he kept them safe-ly in

a pen. Out-side the pen the dogs lay down to guard the flock.

The sheep were hap-py and con-tent-ed. But a fool-ish lit-tle lamb did not like to be shut up, and kept safe-ly. She frown-ed, and pout-ed, and scowl-ed. This naugh-ty lamb came grum-bling to her dam; but her wise mam-ma replied, " You are a sil-ly lamb. If you run a-way you will get in-to harm." But the lamb said to her-self, " I will try to get out." So when the shep-herd led the flock home, she hid her-self in a hole. When the flock were a-sleep she got out, and ran a-bout the hills. But a li-on was prowl-ing a-bout: he saw her. He seiz-ed her in his mouth, and was just go-ing to de-vour her, when the shep-herd shout-ed loud and knock-ed down the li-on with his stout staff. The li-on was a-fraid, and ran a-way howl-ing.

	mount	a-loud
	fount	a-bound
	count	a-round
	coun-ty	fowl-er
Hound	boun-ty	foun-tain
found	coun-ter	moun-tain
sound	thou-sand	found-ling
pound	drought	cow-house

The three dogs in the stable-yard are named Jowl-er, Growl-er, and Howl-er.

The three horses in the sta-ble are named Ram-ble, Scram-ble, and Am-ble.

The three cows in the field are named Spin-dle, Griz-zle, and Spec-kle.

The three cats in the kitch-en are named Catch, Patch, and Scratch.

The three pigs in the sty are named Grum-ble, Mum-ble, and Stum-ble.

Claude wish-ed to have a mouse. But he did not know how to catch a mouse.

Claude was at din-ner in the par-lour with his pa-pa and sis-ters. His sis-ter El-len cried out, "I see a mouse! A lit-tle mouse has just run a-long close by the door!"

Pa-pa cried out, "Now, Claude, catch the mouse if you can."

So Claude got up, and ran a-bout the room. The mouse ran up the curtain, but soon it came down. Claude hunt-ed the mouse till he caught it.

As he held it, his hand was bit-ten by the mouse. Yet he did not let it go. He took it up stairs and kept it in a ba-sin with a net o-ver it.

So he went down a-gain. But when he came up to see his mouse, he found no mouse. It had gnawed the net and got a-way.

Claude was sad, but he did not cry.

our	ow-er	May-flow-er
flour	pow-er	sun-flow-er
sour	bow-er	flow-er-bed
Flow-er	scour	tow-er	flow-er-pot
ow-er our	de-vour	show-er	flow-er-girl

A black man went to a pool with a herd
of cows to give them drink. How much
sur-pri-sed he was to see a li-on ly-ing down
in the pool. He ran a-way quick-ly. The
li-on fol-low-ed him. The li-on did not stop to
de-vour a cow. He li-ked a man bet-ter than
a cow.

The black man scram-bled up a tree with
great speed. The li-on gave a spring at him,
but he had not pow-er to reach him, and he
fell to the ground. He got up quite sour. He
kept go-ing round and round the tree. The
poor fel-low tri-ed to hide him-self from the

li-on a-mong the thick boughs. When he peep-ed to see wheth-er the li-on was wait-ing, he saw the li-on be-low with his eyes fix-ed up-on him, as sour as ev-er.

The li-on lay down be-side the tree That tree was his bow-er, and the black man's tow-er.

Bed-time came, but no bed for the black man; morn-ing came, but no food for him; din-ner-time came, but no din-ner; sup-per-time, but no sup-per. Then it was that the li-on felt so thirs-ty that he rose up and went to a foun-tain. As soon as the poor black man saw the li-on go, he slip-ped down the tree, and ran quick-ly to his house. He reach-ed it in safe-ty. The li-on re-turn-ed to the tree, and when he found the black man had es-cap-ed he fol-low-ed him; but the man got to his house, and shut the door.

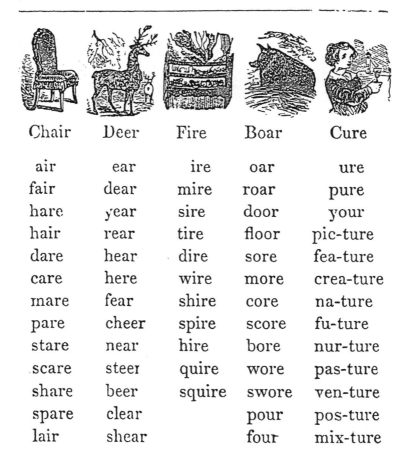

Chair	Deer	Fire	Boar	Cure
air	ear	ire	oar	ure
fair	dear	mire	roar	pure
hare	year	sire	door	your
hair	rear	tire	floor	pic-ture
dare	hear	dire	sore	fea-ture
care	here	wire	more	crea-ture
mare	fear	shire	core	na-ture
pare	cheer	spire	score	fu-ture
stare	near	hire	bore	nur-ture
scare	steer	quire	wore	pas-ture
share	beer	squire	swore	ven-ture
spare	clear		pour	pos-ture
lair	shear		four	mix-ture

A hare is a swift crea-ture. He leaps and gal-lops up the hills so swift-ly that no horse nor dog can o-ver-take him. Men hunt poor lit-tle hares. They gal-lop on hor-ses with dogs, till the hare is tired, and drops down and ex-pires.

A hare lives in a form.

A form is his bed on the ground. He lies in this form du-ring the day, and he feeds in the e-ven-ing in the green pas-tures. In the e-ven-ing hares meet to-geth-er, and play a-bout like chil-dren. They run and leap like mad. crea-tures. But if they hear a sound, they scam-per a-way in a mo-ment. Each hare goes his own way. They can hear the least sound, for they have long ears that can lean every way to catch sounds

A lev-e-ret is a young hare.

Lev-e-rets can be made tame.

Let the Teacher point out that these words are not sounded as they are spelt, but like air.

Bear
there
their
where

Where do bees live? In hives.
Where do rab-bits live? In holes.
Where do bears live? In dens.
Where do birds live? In nests.

Lord Ed-ward went out to shoot bears. He saw a black bear. He shot it, but he did not kill it. He fol-low-ed it, ho-ping to shoot a-gain, but the bear turn-ed round and seiz-ed him with his shag-gy arms. As they strug-gled to-geth-er they fell o-ver the hill-side; but still they went on strug-gling, and Lord Ed-ward went on stab-bing the bear with a dart, and the bear went on bi-ting Lord Ed-ward's arm. The ser-vants made the bear let go. They bore Lord Ed-ward to a house, and laid him on a bed, where he soon di-ed. The bear di-ed of the stabs. His body was found in the road.

Who takes care of your chil-dren? Nurse.
Who scours your floor? The house-maid.
Who rears your flow-ers? The gar-den-er.
Who shears your sheep? The shep-herd.

When El-len was four she was sit-ting in a chair too near the fire. She fell in-to the fire. She seiz-ed the bars of the grate with her lit-tle hands.

O how the dear lit-tle crea-ture did roar!

Nurse was quite near. She ran and lift-ed El-len out of the fire. She found that El-len's lit-tle hands were sad-ly burn-ed. Nurse tri-ed to cure the burns.

El-len must take more care in fu-ture, and not sit so near the fire.

wan	wasp	swal-low
want	what	wal-low
wash	swan	wan-der
was	swamp	watch-man

Watch

NOTE.—*Tell the Child that a after w has the sound of short o, and that* watch *is pronounced as if spelled* "wotch."

Will you go with me to a land far off ?
Yes, I want to go.
What can you do ?
I can milk cows and churn but-ter
What can you do ?
I can plough and reap corn
What can you do ?
I can wash clothes and i-ron them
What can you do ?
I can fell trees and lop off the boughs
What can you do ?
I can build a house and sta-ble.
What can you do ?
I can watch sheep and shear them.

What things shall we take out with us?
I want a milk-pail and a churn.
I want a plough and a sic-kle.
I want a wash-tub and a man-gle.
I want an axe and a saw for the trees.
I want a trow-el and a hod for the bricks.
I want a pair of shears to shear the sheep.
I want a coop for the fowls.
Who will teach the chil-dren? I will.
What shall you want for them?
I shall want a globe, and pens and ink and pa-per, and slates and maps and pic-tures.

Shall you want play-things for the chil-dren?

Yes, I shall want hoops and drums and dolls, play-watch-es and play-guns, hum-ming-tops and skip-ping-ropes, and a rock-ing-horse.

But I shall want more than any-thing— Bi-bles to teach the chil-dren a-bout God and the Lord Je-sus.

boy	spoil	de-stroy
joy	join	en-joy
oil	joint	em-ploy
boil	point	oys-ter
broil	noise	an-oint
coil	a-void	oint-ment

Toys
oy oi oys

" What is this, Char-ley?" said Pa-pa to his boy.
As he spoke he show-ed him a lit-tle box.
He o-pen-ed it and out came a thing like a snake.
It lay coil-ed up up-on the ta-ble.
" It is not a-live," said Char-ley.
" How do you know that?" said his Pa-pa.
" Be-cause a real snake bites. I know it is a
    toy. I am glad it is not a real snake."
Then Char-ley touch-ed the snake.
Here is a doll with joints for Jes-sie.
The doll can bend its arms and legs.
Take care not to de-stroy the doll.
Char-ley, you will not spoil your sis-ter's doll.

A boy went to dine with his grand-pa-pa.
A dish of oys-ters was on the ta-ble.

His grand-pa-pa said, "Those oys-ters were
a-live when they were found on the rocks."

The boy said, "Can they o-pen their own
shells?" "Yes, they can; but they can-not get
out of their shells. They do not want to get out."

"Then why do they o-pen their shells?"

"To let the sea flow in, for they drink the
sea; it is their food : it keeps them a-live."

What is the mat-ter with that lit-tle boy?

He has taken poi-son. He saw a cup of
poi-son on the shelf. He said, "This seems
sweet stuff." So he drank it.

Can the doc-tor cure him? No. Will the
poi-son de-stroy him? Yes, he must die.

NOTE.—*Children may now read any little books, such as
"Tiny Stories." Variety will hasten their progress.*

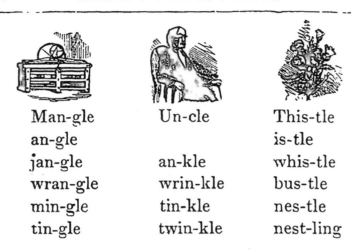

Man-gle	Un-cle	This-tle
an-gle		is-tle
jan-gle	an-kle	whis-tle
wran-gle	wrin-kle	bus-tle
min-gle	tin-kle	nes-tle
tin-gle	twin-kle	nest-ling

NOTE.—*These words have the sounds of* ing *and* ang, *and* sl'.

Ra-chel and Su-san liv-ed in a coun-try house. When they o-pen-ed their win-dow in the morn-ing they saw the bough of a high birch-tree. In the spring a pair of rob-ins būilt their nest on that bough. The two sis-ters watch-ed the birds build-ing their lit-tle nests. They li-ked so much to see them with lit-tle bits of moss or hay in their beaks.

Then they saw the hen-rob-in sit-ting day by day, hatch-ing her eggs, while she lis-ten-ed to the sweet songs of her mate. There was much bus-tle when the lit-tle nest-lings came out of the eggs. The rob-ins has-ten-ed to get them food. The hun-gry nest-lings o-pen-ed wide their mouths to take in the food. There were two lit-tle birds in the nest for the two big birds to take care of.

Ra-chel and Su-san werē in the gar-den with their Un-cle.. The rob-ins made a great noise that day. They seem-ed to be an-gry with the girls and their un-cle for ap-proach-ing the tree. They came down to the low-est boughs. They chat-ter-ed loud, and flit-ted to and fro as if they were wrang-ling and jang-ling with ev-e-ry bo-dy.

The wind had blown hard, and the Un-cle fear-ed that the nest was spoil-ed. So he

went with the girls to see whe-ther the nest-
lings had tum-bled out

They soon found the lit-tle birds on the
ground. The first bird had a bro-ken leg, and
the next bird had been kil-led. The Un-cle
lift-ed up the first bird, and held it in his
hand. He said to the girls, "I will try to
mend this bro-ken leg."

So he got strips of lin-en and ti-ed them
round the bird's bod-y, and bound up the
ti-ny bro-ken leg.

But how did the big birds like this med-
dling with their dear nest-ling? They were
so an-gry! They fol-low-ed the Un-cle to the
door of the house, cry-ing an-gri-ly, and fly-ing
just o-ver him; but they were a-fraid to go
in-to the house.

When the Un-cle had ti-ed up the bro-ker
leg, he re-turn-ed out of doors with the nest

ling in his hand. He laid it down on a lit-tle tuft of hay. There he left it.

Its Pa-pa and Mam-ma soon saw it, and came and fed it. The Un-cle felt much joy when he saw the nest-ling was fed. Lit-tle Pa-pa and Mam-ma tri-ed to make the lit-tle fel-low fly up in-to its nest in the tree. But the lit-tle bird was not a-ble to fly, for its wings were too weak for fly-ing; and they werē ti-ed down with strips of lin-en. It was of no use for Pa-pa and Mam-ma to hop and to chirp and to whis-tle,—poor wee bir-die was not a-ble to stir.

Those poor birds had no more nest-lings now, and they were much griev-ed to lose this lit-tle dar-ling.

It be-gan to rain soon. The Un-cle did not like to leave wee bir-die out in the rain and in the dark, and so he pick-ed it up, and nurs-ed it at home. He fed it. He was pleas-ed to see the bird o-pen its beak, and take in the food.

Next morn-ing the Un-cle wish-ed the big birds to see it a-gain; but they had left the tree, and flown far a-way. So they saw their nest-ling no more.

The Un-cle went on feed-ing it. The bird got bet-ter and bet-ter. In six weeks the Un-cle un-did the strips, and let the bird stand. He was glad to see it stand near-ly straight.

He ex-pect-ed his bird to fly a-way now, and re-turn to its friends in the trees. He let the door of the house be o-pen, and the win-dows too. But bir-die did not go out It li-ked bet-ter fly-ing a-bout the house, and perch-ing on the backs of the chairs, and hop-ping on the ta-bles. Still more it lik-ed to sit on the Un-cle's back. So from this time the bird be-came the pet of the fam-i-ly, and had the name of Bob-bit giv-en to it.

When the Un-cle goes in-to the gar-den, Bob-bit goes with him.   It flies from his back to seek for in-sects in the ground.   If it hear the least noise, or bus-tle, it has-tens back to the house.

Ev-e-ry morn-ing it goes out a-lone to seek for in-sects a-mong the flow-er-beds.   It pecks the ground with its beak, and drags out a grub or bee-tle for its din-ner.

When it is thirs-ty it goes to the pipe in the kit-chen to drink.   A dish is set up-on the ground for it to wash in.   When it has bath-ed, it perch-es on the rail-ing to dry it-self in the sun.   When it is hot—it hides it-self in a tree.

When the Un-cle miss-es it, he goes in-to the gar-den to seek it.   He cries out, " Bob-bit,

Bob-bit!" Bob-bit soon re-plies by a chirp or a whis-tle.

When it is ev-en-ing Bob-bit re-turns home. It has fix-ed on a spot to sleep in. This spot is in Un-cle's stud-y, on the top of his cab-in-et. There he sleeps qui-et-ly, with his head un-der his wing, un-til the morn-ing dawns.

Bob-bit has lit-tle play-fel-lows in the gar-den. Who are the play-fel-lows?

Un-cle was sit-ting in the par-lour, when he saw Bob-bit with four rob-ins. They seem-ed to have a great deal to say to Bob-bit. Un-cle sup-pos-ed they wer̄e beg-ging Bob-bit to go a-way with them; but the four rob-ins went a-way, and Bob-bit came in-to the par-loūr and perch-ed on the back of Un-cle's chair.

There is a cat in the house, and this cat u-sed to stare at Bob-bit, and seem-ed to be long-ing to eat him up; but when-ev-er Ra-chel and Su-san saw the cat watch-ing Bob-bit, they hunt-ed her a-way, and made such a noise, that now the cat is a-fraid of med-dling with Bob-bit, and ne-ver seems to see him when she meets him in the house, or in the gar-den.

So Bob-bit leads a hap-py life.

Bob-bit is fond of Ra-chel and Su-san, for they have ta-ken much care of him; but he is fond-er of the Un-cle, for he has tak-en still more care of him. He shows his fond-ness by fol-low-ing him from room to room, by stay-ing be-side him in the gar-den, and by sit-ting on his desk for hours to-ge-ther. He nev-er seems ti-red of watch-ing his friend while he is wri-ting. He waits and waits till this dear friend has fin-ish-ed his let-ters, and can go with him in-to the gar-den

NOTE — *Tell the Child that* ow *and* ou *are some-times sounded like long* o.

To bow		A bow
how	bowl	to sow
now	soul	to mow
cow	wid-ow	to know
sow	win-dow	to throw
Thou	pil-low	to stow
bough	bil-low	to be-stow
plough	wil-low	crow
drown	bel-low	snow
brown	yel-low	low
cloud	fel-low	low-er
shroud	hol-low	low-est
howl	tal-low	low-ly
growl	own	mow-er
found	own-er	thrown
ground	flown	known

Did you ev-er hear of the don-key that went in-to the sea with .the lit-tle cart?

Tell me, Mam-ma, how it was that the don-key did so.

Well, my dear, this was the way. A la-dy drove the cart down to the beach. She had six chil-dren with her. Three lit-tle ones sat in the cart by her side. Three big-ger girls ran be-fore the cart.

When they came to the beach, the la-dy and the chil-dren got out.

The la-dy wish-ed the don-key to bathe its legs in the sea, to make it strong and clean. But the don-key did not like to go near the sea. So the la-dy bound a brown shawl o-ver its eyes, and she bade the big girls lead it close to the waves. Sud-den-ly a big wave rush-ed on to the land. The girls start-ed back to a-void the wave, and they let go the don-key's rein.

The don-key was a-larm-ed by the noise the girls made, and it went in-to the sea, not know-ing where it was go-ing be-cause it was not a-ble to see. The girls ran scream-ing to the la-dy, cry-ing out, "The don-key is in the sea!"

There it was, go-ing fur-ther and fur-ther in-to the sea, drag-ging the cart a-long, till the cart was hid-den by the bil-lows. The don-key sank low-er and low-er ev-e-ry mo-ment, till no part of it was seen but the ears; for the brown shawl was o-ver its nose and mouth.

Now the chil-dren be-gan to bawl and to bel-low! But no one hal-loo-ed so loud as the lit-tle boy of four   His name was Mer-ty. He fear-ed that the don-key was drown-ed

No boat was near that day, but there were boats far a-way. Two fish-er-men were in a boat far a-way They said, "We hear howls and shrieks on the shore. Per-haps a boy or girl is drown-ing. Let us go and save him." So they row-ed hard, and they soon came to the poor don-key, and saw its ears peep-ing out of the sea. The don-key was just go-ing to sink when they lift-ed it up by its jaws, and seiz-ed the bri-dle and drag-ged it a-long. The chil-dren on the shore shout-ed a-loud for joy. The don-key with the cart came safe to land. The poor crea-ture was weak, and drip-ping wet. The fish-er-men un-bound its eyes, and said to the la-dy, "We can-not think how this thing came to be o-ver its eyes." The la-dy said she wish-ed she had not bound up its eyes, and she gave the shillings in her purse to the fish-er-men who had sa-ved her don-key.

NOTE.—*Let the Child be told that many words of two syllables in spelling are pronounced as one syllable—such as* stop-ped, *which is pronounced* stopt.

Rub	The maid rub-bed the ta-ble.
Rob	A rob-ber rob-bed the tra-vel-ler.
Sob	The ba-by sob-bed it-self to sleep
Stab	A wretch stab-bed a king.
Crack	A lad crack-ed nuts.
Peck	The fowls peck-ed the bar-ley
Lick	The dog lick-ed my hand.
Kick	The horse kick-ed the groom.
Prick	The pin prick-ed the ba-by.
Tick	The clock tick-ed loud.
Lock	Rich-ard lock-ed up his desk.
Knock	A vis-it-or knock-ed at the door.
Rock	Su-san rock-ed the cra-dle.
Pluck	My sis-ter pluck-ed this ap-ple.
Tuck	Mam-ma tuck-ed me up in bed.
Lap	The cat lap-ped up the milk.

Strap	The por-ter strap-ped up my trunk.
Clap	Lit-tle Ar-thur clap-ped his hands.
Step	I step-ped o-ver the stream.
Whip	Tom was whip-ped for tell-ing a lie.
Skip	Lau-ra skip-ped on the lawn.
Dip	Nurse dip-ped me in the sea.
Hop	The rob-in hop-ped on the ta-ble.
Mop	Sal-ly mop-ped up the kit-chen.
Crop	The hair-dress-er crop-ped Dicky's hair.
Stop	We stop-ped at an inn on the way.
Pop	My Un-cle pop-ped in at six o'clock.
Wag	Pom-pey wag-ged his tail at the gate.
Beg	Tom-my beg-ged for a crust.
Jog	Frank jog-ged me when I wrote.
Hug	A bear hug-ged the man till he di-ed.
Tug	Three men tug-ged the boat to land.
Pin	Nurse pin-ned my shawl.
Skin	A man skin-ned the rab-bit.
Hem	Fan-ny hem-med ba-by's pin-a-fore.

A lit-tle boy liv-ed near a high moun-tain.
He saw the top reach-ing to the clouds, and he
wish-ed to go up.   But his Pa-pa for-bid him
to go up.   He said he was too young and too
weak to go up such a high moun-tain.   But
the lit-tle boy still wish-ed to go up.

His Pa-pa and Mam-ma left home to spend
the day out.   They left him un-der the care of
a ser-vant.   But the ser-vant had plen-ty to
do, and the boy got a-way with-out her miss-ing
him.   They said to him, "Dear Ar-thur, we
can-not take you with us, for we shall not
re-turn till quite late.   Su-san the maid will
take care of you while we are out, and give
you din-ner and sup-per, and help you to go
to bed.   You may play in the gar-den, but
you must not go out of the gate."

Ar-thur prom-is-ed to o-bey.   At first he
play-ed in the gar-den.   He came in at din-ner-

time, and then went out a-gain to play. He got tir-ed of play-ing a-lone. He be-gan to wish to go up the moun-tain. So he watch-ed till Su-san went up-stairs to wash her hands and brush her hair. He said to him-self, " I will slip a-way be-fore she returns." He got his hat and his great coat, and his Pa-pa's stick. Then he slip-ped out at the door, and shut it quiet-ly. Then with the strong stick in his hand he be-gan to go up the steep mountain.

He came at first to green moss and pink and pur-ple flowers ; but as he got high-er, he saw no more flow-ers. He went on for hours, till he was quite tir-ed and faint; but he seem-ed as far as ev-er from the top. He sat down to rest He found him-self quite a-lone. Not a sheep nor a shep-herd was to be seen. Soon a big flake of snow from the moun-tain side came down and fell up-on his dress. More snow came, and more snow, till there was snow every-where.

Now the boy was a-fraid in-deed. Now he began to fear he must sleep on the moun-tain side up-on the snow. He felt how naugh-ty it was to dis-o-bey his Pa-pa, and he fear-ed that God was an-gry with him.

He tri-ed to get down, but he did not re-mem-ber which way he came up. He cri-ed aloud, but no-bod-y was near. He sank in the snow at each step. The tears flow-ed from his eyes, and froze up-on his cheeks.

He knelt down up-on the snow, and sob-bed out a pray-er to God.

He said, " O God, for-give my sin, and do not let me die on this moun-tain. Pit-y my Pa-pa and Mam-ma ; and do not let them have the grief of los-ing me."

Soon he fell a-sleep in the dark, with snow

for his pil-low. He must have di-ed in his sleep had he stay-ed long on his snow-y bed.

Sud-den-ly he felt a touch. He felt a crea-ture breathe up-on his cheek. He start-ed up and scream-ed; and now he saw a fine, big, black and white dog, stand-ing be-side him. This dog did not wish to hurt him, but was try-ing to make him well.

The dog lick-ed the boy, breath-ed on him, rub-bed him with his hair-y coat, and show-ed him a lit-tle keg of bran-dy ti-ed round his neck. The boy drank a lit-tle of it, and found him-self much bet-ter. But he was still too weak to get up the moun-tain, so he got on the dog's shag-gy back.

This dear dog crawl-ed up the moun-tain with his big bur-den, till he came to a house where men liv-ed. These men lift-ed the poor boy in-to the house, and nurs-ed him in their arms.

They laid him on a neat bed. Then they boil-ed a lit-tle milk and gave it to Ar-thur to sip.

As soon as Ar-thur was a-ble to speak he thank-ed the men for sav-ing his life by send-ing out the dog.

The men said, " Tell us the names of your Pa-pa and Mam-ma, that we may send for them."

Ar-thur was a-ble to say what their names were.

So the men sent for them.

When they came they said to Ar-thur, "We have not slept, nor eat-en, nor drank. We have wept and cri-ed for our dear boy."

" Oh, for-give me !" said Ar-thur, with tears. " Oh, may God for-give me for not o-bey-ing you, my dear Pa-pa and Mam-ma."

Note.—-*These* past tenses *are to be pronounced as one syllable.*

stain	stained	nurse	nursed
clean	cleaned	darn	darned
smile	smiled	whirl	whirled
hope	hoped	clothe	clothed
moan	moaned	breathe	breathed
groan	groaned	stamp	stamped
tune	tuned	jump	jumped
like	liked	chirp	chirped
croak	croaked	choke	choked
nail	nailed	loose	loosed
dream	dreamed	fetch	fetched
foam	foamed	snatch	snatched
show	showed	pinch	pinched
brush	brushed	stoop	stooped
fish	fished	smooth	smoothed
whine	whined	gnaw	gnawed
wheel	wheeled	crawl	crawled

share	shared	whis-per	whis-pered
fear	feared	thun-der	thun-dered
tire	tired	fol-low	fol-lowed
roar	roared	fin-ish	fin-ished
care	cared	ga-ther	gath-ered
boil	boiled	mur-mur	mur-mured
dine	dined	grum-ble	grum-bled
join	joined	scat-ter	scat-tered
milk	milked	con-fess	con-fessed
peep	peeped	par-don	par-doned
play	played	dis-please	dis-pleased
plough	ploughed	em-ploy	em-ployed
praise	praised	en-joy	en-joyed
preach	preached	a-muse	a-mused
tease	teased	de-sire	de-sired
thank	thanked	o-bey	o-beyed
try	tried	ap-pear	ap-peared
watch	watched	lis-ten	lis-tened
yawn	yawned	wan-der	wan-dered

A la-dy went out to buy things at shops. She came back with a num-ber of things in her big bag. There was rib-bon for her own bon-net, and lit-tle shoes for ba-by, and pic-tures for her lit-tle Ed-win.

But Ed-win did not meet her at the door. When he saw his Mam-ma, he did not run to her.

She said to him, "I hope you have en-joy-ed your-self while I was out."

But Ed-win made no re-ply. He did not fol-low Mam-ma up-stairs, but ran in-to the gar-den. Mam-ma was sur-pris-ed, for Ed-win used to be fond of her. She saw him out of win-dow, and nod-ded to him, but he seem-ed not to see her.

When bed-time came his Mam-ma un dress-ed him. He said to her, "Mam-ma, can God see through a crack in the cup-board?"

"Oh, yes!" re-pli-ed Mam-ma.

" And can He see when it is quite dark there ?" said Ed-win.

" Oh, yes !" re-pli-ed Mam-ma. " God can see every-where."

" Then," said Ed-win, " God saw me, and I will tell you, Mam-ma. When you were gone out to-day I went in-to your cup-board and ate up the cake. I am very un-hap-py—very un-hap-py." Then he bow-ed down on his Mam-ma's lap, and burst out cry-ing.

Poor lit-tle boy! he had tri-ed to hide him-self from his Mam-ma, as Ad-am and Eve hid them-selves from God. But now he had con-fess-ed his sin, and he did not wish to hide him-self any more. Now he nest-led close to his Mam-ma. She for-gave him, and kiss-ed him. Ed-win knelt down at her knees and pray-ed to God to wash a-way his sins, for Je-sus' sake.

NOTE.—*Let the Teacher tell the Child that words ending in* t *or* d *cannot in the past tense be pronounced as one syllable.*

Pat	Het-ty pat-ted the spot-ted kit-ten.
Plat	Kit-ty plat-ted straw for a bon-net.
Chat	Pat-ty chat-ted too much at din-ner.
Fat	Bid-dy has fat-ted the pig.
Add	Pa-pa has ad-ded a bit to my gar-den.
Pad	I have fit-ted on my pad-ded coat.
Mud	A rude boy mud-ded it in sport.
Fade	My rose fa-ded in an hour.
Shade	A tree sha-ded me from the sun
Braid	Mam-ma braid-ed my jack-et.
Load	Jack load-ed his wag-gon with hay.
Bait	He bait-ed the hor-ses on the way.
Wait	I wait-ed a long while for the train.
Hate	Wick-ed Cain ha-ted A-bel.
Grate	Nurse gra-ted nut-meg in my gru-el.
Treat	She treat-ed me ten-der-ly when I was ill.
Heat	She heat-ed my tea in the lamp.

Doat	She doat-ed on me when I was a babe
Cheat	Rich-ard was cheat-ed at the shop.
Cart	The hay was cart-ed on Sat-ur-day.
Start	I start-ed when my un-cle came in.
Dart	He dart-ed sud-den-ly in-to the room.
Dust	Bes-sy dust-ed the room quick-ly.
Rust	The knife was rust-ed by the rain.
Land	The sail-ors land-ed be-fore the storm.
Mend	Han-nah mend-ed her clothes neat-ly.
Pelt	The boys pelt-ed me with snow.
Melt	The snow has melt-ed a-way.
Haste	When I cri-ed John hast-ed to my help
Feast	The school feast-ed on the lawn.
Waste	Not a bit of food was wast-ed.
Roast	Tom roast-ed his ches-nuts by my fire.
Toast	He toast-ed cheese for his sup-per.
Boast	He boast-ed of his skill in fish-ing.
Cord	Sam cord-ed my box for the train.
Hoard	Ben hoard-ed nuts in his cup-board.

THE LIT-TLE FISH-ER.

Sam was the least of the fam-i-ly: so h
was the pet and the dar-ling. And he was a
boy who did as he was bid; and this made
him a dar-ling.

There was a lake near his Pa-pa's house.
The lake was deep. Sam's Pa-pa was a-fraid
of his dear boy be-ing drown-ed. So he for-bid
him to go a-lone to the lake.

Sam beg-ged his Pa-pa to let him go there
fish-ing next Sat-ur-day with three boys.

His Pa-pa was a lit-tle a-fraid to let him go

Sam prom-is-ed to take great care.

" Well," said his Pa-pa, " you may go this
time; but pray do take care."

Sam jump-ed for joy and said, " I shall
bring you home a long string of fish for
sup-per, if—if—if—I re-turn home safe."

"But," said his Pa-pa, "you must make up fag-ots on Sat-ur-day morn-ing be-fore you go fish-ing."

"Oh, yes!" said the lit-tle boy; "I like to help you, dear Pa-pa!"

Sam count-ed the days till Sat-ur-day came.

On Sat-ur-day morn-ing he cut up sticks, and ti-ed them in bun-dles. Be-fore he had fin-ish-ed—three lit-tle boys came to the house to fetch him. Sam said, "Wait till I have fin-ish-ed my fag-ots." Then Sam ran for his fish-ing-rod and his lit-tle pail.

The four lit-tle boys ran ea-ger-ly down to the lake. There was a long pier on the lake. The boys ran quick-ly a-long the pier. When they reach-ed the end of the pier they let down their fish-ing-rods. They soon caught fish-es. Each time that they found a fish at the end of the rod they felt much pleas-ed.

They had caught a num-ber of fish-es by six o'clock. They wish-ed to re-turn home. They had join-ed their fish to-geth-er with a string. Each boy had a string of fish to take home.

"Where is my string of fish?" said Sam. "Have you seen it?"

The boys said they had not seen it.

"Oh!" said Sam, "I can-not go home with-out my fish-es. I must stay till I have found it, or till I have got more fish-es." So Sam's three friends went home, and Sam stay-ed on the pier.

It was fool-ish of Sam to stay a-lone on the pier, for if Sam were to slip into the riv-er he must be drown-ed.

That e-ven-ing Sam was seen stand-ing at the end of the pier fish-ing a-lone, and he was nev-er seen a-gain. Per-haps he tri-ed to get

out his string of fish, and so slip-ped in-to the
riv-er.

His Mam-ma at home saw it was get-ting
dark. She sent his sis-ter to fetch Sam home.
But his sis-ter did not re-turn. Soon Sam's
Pa-pa went to the lake with his friends. But
he saw no Sam. He found Sam's fish-ing-rod
and his pail on the pier; but no Sam-my.

Men drag-ged up his lit-tle bod-y from the
bot-tom of the lake. A great num-ber of chil-
dren came to the fu-ne-ral, and saw the lit-tle
bod-y laid in the grave.

But where was Sam-my's soul? With God
in the sky.

Sam was a boy who be-liev-ed in Je-sus,
and pray-ed to Him, when he was quite a-lone.
Pa-pa and Mam-ma have wept bit-ter-ly for
their dar-ling, but they know they shall meet
him in the sky.

NOTE.—*Let the Teacher explain to the Child that the last Syllable in these words is scarcely heard, and the vowel almost dropped.*

ta-ken	sev-en	ba-sin
sha-ken	sad-den	ma-son
wa-ken	glad-den	bur-den
ra-ven	cho-sen	cot-ton
bro-ken	fro-zen	kit-ten
spo-ken	hid-den	but-ton
eat-en	bid-den	mut-ton
beat-en	ris-en	rai-sin
giv-en	writ-ten	rea-son
driv-en	bit-ten	sea-son
hap-pen	ri-pen	les-son

Little Bet-sy did not like to read her les-son. When her Mam-ma was go-ing to teach her she fret-ted and said, "I wish I was a kit-ten; be-cause kit-tens have no les-sons."

"Well," said her Mam-ma, "you may be

a kit-ten, if you please ; but if you play like a kit-ten you must live like a kit-ten."

Bet-sy clap-ped her hands for joy. "How hap-py I shall be to-day!" said Bet-sy.

Then she ran in-to the gar-den to play. At din-ner time she came in with her frock quite dir-ty. She ran to her Mam-ma; but her Mam-ma cried out, "Get a-way, dir-ty kit-ten!"

Din-ner was laid on the ta-ble, but there was no chair for Bet-sy. Mam-ma said, "The cats and the kit-tens are fed in the kit-chen." So Bet-sy went in-to the kit-chen for her food. The maids gave her sop in a plate up-on the floor.

Bet-sy saw her Mam-ma in her bon-net, go-ing to pay a vis-it. She said, "May I go, too?" "No," said her Mam-ma: "I nev-er take kit-tens out with me." That even-ing Bet-sy said, "I do not wish to be a kit-ten any long-er. I had soon-er do very long less-ons a-gain."

NOTE.—Let the Child be again reminded that words beginning with the vowels a e i o u have an instead of a placed before them.

An an-i-mal	An a-bode
An elk	An al-ley
An eel	An out-house
An owl	An or-chard
An asp	An ap-ple
An ea-gle	An a-pri-cot
An ot-ter	An el-der tree
An em-met	An arch
An oys-ter	An oar
An egg	An an-vil
An arm	An i-dol
An eye	An ink-stand
An ear	An em-e-rald
An an-kle	An in-stru-ment
An el-bow	An ar-my
An a-pron	An en-e-my
An om-ni-bus	An un-cle

An o-be-di-ent boy
An an-gry dog
An i-dle school-boy
An ill-na-tur-ed play-fel-low
An ob-sti-nate girl
An en-vi-ous en-e-my
An un-hap-py per-son
An at-ten-tive pu-pil
An im-pu-dent lad
An ig-no-rant man
An ug-ly pup-py
An i-vo-ry box
An e-bo-ny ink-stand
An un-ripe peach
An up-per room
An un-der-ground rail-way
An awk-ward por-ter
An emp-ty trunk
An ab-sent friend

THE BIRTH-DAY.

Ber-tie was so glad when his birth-day
came! He had spo-ken a-bout it a long
time. He a-woke soon in the morn-ing and
said, "It is my birth-day." Nurse said,
"Thank God for hav-ing kept you a-live for
five years, and made you so strong and well."
Pa-pa came in-to the room to kiss Ber-tie. But
Pa-pa was go-ing to spend the day far a-way.
He said, "I shall re-turn late, and I will bring
home pic-tures for my boy." Ber-tie was not
a-ble to read yet, but he li-ked pic-tures.

When Ber-tie was dress-ed he went to his
Mam-ma's room to say his prayers. He came
down-stairs with a wreath of flow-ers in his
hair. Such sweet flow-ers were in the wreath.
There were red and white rose-buds, and
green leaves.

Ber-tie held a pres-ent in his hand. It was a paint-box his Mam-ma had giv-en him, with brush-es and lit-tle plates in-side. Ber-tie was much pleas-ed to see red and blue and yel-low paints. He wish-ed to sit down and paint that mo-ment; but Grand-mam-ma said, " You have no time to paint now." So Ber-tie went up-stairs to pre-pare for go-ing to Cro-mer.

The don-key came to the door. Ber-tie rode on it, and lit-tle Char-ley rode too. Char-ley had a sad-dle like a chair, and he was tied in it. Ber-tie did not wish to be tied; for he was much big-ger than Char-ley.

Six poor chil-dren ran by the side of the don-key. Cou-sin Su-san came with them. She was a big girl, who was fond of play-ing with lit-tle chil-dren.

The chil-dren hop-ed to go in a boat on the sea—but when they came to the sea-side they were sur-pris-ed to see the waves quite high and foam-ing. The boat was there, but it kept far a-way from the beach. The boat-man lift-ed up his hat, as much as to say, " You can-not get in-to my boat."

So Ber-tie and Char-ley were led home on the don-key. Mam-ma was there with the car and the white po-ny, and she drove Char-ley to Cro-mer. Cou-sin Su-san had a don-key cart, and she drove Ber-tie to Cro-mer. Grand-mam-ma led the poor chil-dren with her to Cro-mer, by the cliff. They had the don-key to ride when they were tir-ed, and they rode by turns. When they got to Cro-mer, they found little Ber-tie and Char-ley there with Mam-ma and Cou-sin Su-san.

They went first to a shop, and had cakes. Then they went down to the pier, or jet-ty. They li-ked run-ning on it, and feel-ing the

wind blow, and see-ing the waves be-low.
Then they went to a toy-shop. Each of the
poor chil-dren had a case with a pen in-side.
Ber-tie had a big wheel to run be-fore him,
and Char-ley had a lit-tle white dog.

They re-turn-ed home for din-ner.

When din-ner was o-ver Ber-tie a-mus-ed
him-self in paint-ing pic-tures.

At four o'clock it was time to go to the
hills, to take tea there. The maids bring
ket-tles and cans, and cups, and plates, and
loaves, and but-ter, and tea, and milk, and
jam. They load the don-key cart with these
things. Then Ber-tie and Char-ley get in and
go to the hills. The whole par-ty go too.
They do not wish to ride, for the hills are near.

When they get to the spot they take the
don-key out of the cart, and tie him to a tree
with a rope.

Then the chil-dren gath-er stones to pre-
pare for the fire. Then they pick up sticks and
fir-cones, and they lay them on the stones.
Soon the fire is burn-ing up, and the two ket-
tles are in the flames. When the ket-tles boil
they are fill-ed with tea. The tea-things are
laid on the ground, and the whole par-ty sit on
the ground. The nurse is there with ba-by.
The num-ber of peōple is twen-ty.

Each hands a cup to be fill-ed with tea and
milk. Ba-by sips milk, and eats lit-tle bits of
the loaf with but-ter. There is jam for those
who like it, and there is a plain cake.

The chil-dren sing a verse of thanks be-fore
they be-gin to eat.

Tea is o-ver. Su-san runs down the hill to
play in a hay-field. The chil-dren run with her,
and play at ma-ny games. They join hands,
and go round in a ring, sing-ing as they go.

They hide and seek; they run and catch. Ber-tie says, " I want you to play at my game."

They re-ply, " We will, be-cause it is your birth-day.   What is your game?"

" It is play-ing at go-ing in a train." So Ber-tie tells each to stand near a hay-cock; and he him-self stands near a hay-cock and jumps, and cries out the names of the towns. The rest are soon tired of this game, though Ber-tie likes it so much.

It is time for the chil-dren to go home.

Now the don-key must be un-tied that he may draw the lit-tle cart home.   The maid packs up the cans and ket-tles, the cups and plates, the knives and spoons.   But she has no milk nor but-ter, no cake nor jam, to pack up.

Ber-tie's Pa-pa brings him pic-tures as he prom-is-ed.   Mam-ma tells Ber-tie to thank God for giv-ing him such a hap-py birth-day

	old	on't	own
	cold	don't	grown
Colt	gold	won't	flown
olt	sold		shown
bolt	hold	ome	
moūlt	fold	comb	only
	bold		
oll	told	oath	ost
roll		both	host
toll	old-er	loth	most
soul	bold-er	sloth	post
whole	cold-er		roast
	mould-er		
oak	smould-er		coast
yolk	shoul-der		boast
folks	sol-di-er		toast

A colt is a young horse.
A foal is a young don-key.
A pig is a young hog.
A lamb̄ is a young sheep.
A pup-py is a young dog.
A kit-ten is a young cat.
A chick-en is a young hen.
An ea-glet is a young ea-gle.
A cub is a young bear or li-on.
A boy is a young man.
A fold is for sheep.   A nest is for birds
A form is for hares.   A hole is for rats.
A den is for li-ons.   A sta-ble is for hors-es.
A ken-nel is for dogs.   A hive is for bees.
A nur-se-ry is for chil-dren.
Where is gold found?   Un-der-ground
Where is sil-ver found?   Un-der-ground.
Where is cop-per found?   Un-der-ground.
Where is iron found?   Un-der-ground

NOTE.— *The i in the following words is sounded long, as in* ice.

ind	rind	un-kind
Child	mind	grind	kind-ness
ild	find	blind	blind-ness
wild	kind	pint	wild-ness
mild	bind	climb	be-hind

In the following words gh *is not sounded, and the* i *is long.*

night	fight	de-light
light	bright	light-en
sight	might	bright-en
slight	fright	fright-en

Ma-bel went to see Grand-mam-ma. She vent in the coach. There was no train. She went quite a-lone. The dri-ver of the coach stop-ped his hor-ses at Grand-mam-ma's door with the box-es. Ma-bel had two box-es: a box for her own clothes, and a box for a cap to give Grand-mam-ma. Ma-bel had made the cap with her own hands. Grand-mam-ma came smil-ing to the door. She kiss-ed the child, and spoke kind-ly to her. Ma-bel soon show-ed Grand-mam-ma the cap, and beg-ged her to try it on. Grand-mam-ma found it fit-ted her well, and she thank-ed Ma-bel for her kind pres-ent.

When night came—Ma-bel was sleep-y. Grand-mam-ma led her to a lit-tle room close to her own. The bed had white cur-tains, the car-pet was blue, and the pa-per was paint-ed with pink rose-buds. Ma-bel was de-light-ed with the room; and she un-dress-ed quick-ly and went to bed. But Ma-bel did not go to sleep for a long while.

When Grand-mam-ma came up to bed she found Ma-bel a-sleep; but she was sur-pris-ed

to see a tear up-on her cheek She saw Ma-bel
had cri-ed her-self to sleep.

Next day Grand-mam-ma said to Ma-bel,
"At night I saw a tear on your cheek. Had
you cri-ed be-cause you want-ed to go home?"

"Oh, no!" said Ma-bel; "I do not want
to go home yet. I am quite hap-py here."

"Then why did you cry?" said Grand-
mam-ma. But Ma-bel did not tell her why.

Next night Grand-mam-ma saw the same
tear-drop on the child's cheek, and the next
night too.

So the next night Grand-mam-ma did not
go down-stairs, but sat in her own room to
see what was the mat-ter with Ma-bel. Soon
the child be-gan to move a-bout the bed, and
to give a lit-tle cry and a loud sob. Then
Grand-mam-ma went in-to the lit-tle girl's
room with a light in her hand. She found

her a-wake in her bed. She said to her, " My dear child, you must have a thorn in your pil-low.'

What did she mean by a thorn? Her mean-ing was, Ma-bel is think-ing of a sad thing, that pricks her heart like a thorn.

Ma-bel hid her burn-ing cheeks un-der the pil-low, and burst out cry-ing.

" What can be the mat-ter?" said Grand-mam-ma.

" Oh, Grand-mam-ma!" said Ma-bel, " when I am a-lone here I can-not help think-ing of what I said to Mam-ma be-fore I left home. I said, ' I won't.' And Mam-ma is so kind, and I was so naugh-ty." Then the tears flow-ed a-fresh down the child's cheeks. Grand-mam-ma kiss-ed lit-tle Ma-bel, and said, " Ask God to for-give you for Jesus' sake, and He will blot out your sin."

K

NOTE.—*In the words below* ou *is sounded like* u.

cous-in	trouble	jour-ney
coun-try	double	young

Ber-tha and Mar-tha were to go on a jour-ney with Pa-pa. They were much pleas-ed.

Nurse woke them in the dark, and dress-ed them quick-ly. She led them down-stairs, and told them to get in-to the fly. Mam-ma kiss-ed them be-fore they got in; but she was too weak and ill to take a long jour-ney. A young cous-in of five years old went with Ber-tha and Mar-tha. She was a lit-tle young-er than Mar-tha. Her name was Kate.

Ber-tha was the old-est. She was sev-en. Pa-pa let Mar-tha sit on his knee. Nurse let the lit-tle cous-in sit on her knee, and Ber-tha sat be-tween Nurse and Pa-pa.

Soon the light be-gan to shine.

Pa-pa said to the chil-dren, "This is the coun-try." The chil-dren saw green fields ; but the trees had no leaves, for it was win-ter.

It was quite dark when they got to Grand-pa-pa s house.

Next day they play-ed a-bout the house. Mar-tha liked to be with her cous-in, and to do every-thing that Kate did.

Kate said to Mar-tha, " Let us take the hats and whips, and play at ma-king a house." So they laid the hats and the whips on the floor, and be-gan to whip the floor with whips. Nurse found them, and was an-gry with Mar-tha. She said, "You give double trouble to the maids by throw-ing a-bout the hats !"

Nurse said to Kate—"You are younger than your cous-in, and that is your excuse!" Martha felt ashamed, but still she went on doing the same foolish things as her cousin.

NOTE.—*Let the Teacher tell the Child that o sometimes has the sound of* u.

	un	uth (*soft*)	uth (*hard*)
	won	doth	oth-er
Dove	one	nothing	moth-er
ove	sun	ung	broth-er
love	done	tongue	uz
shove	mon-ey	a-mong	does
shov-el	hon-ey	monkey	doz-en

Rose, Jes-sy, and Lil-y lived in a pret-ty coun-try house. One day Pa-pa came in-to the nur-se-ry and said, "Dear chil-dren, God has sent you a ba-by broth-er."

Pa-pa led the chil-dren one by one to see the ba-by broth-er. He was ly-ing in the nurse's lap, and was cov-er-ed up with flan-nel.

That day the chil-dren spoke of nothing but their lit-tle broth-er. When they went in-to the lane, they ran up and down sing-ing, " We have a lit-tle broth-er."

The ba-by's moth-er lov-ed him much.

She said he was her love, her dove, her dar-ling son, her hon-ey-bee, and her heart's cere-fort. She laid him on the so-fa to sleep, and cov-er-ed him with her brown shawl.

While the ba-by was a-sleep his sis-ters went a-bout on tip-toe, for fear they might wake him.

Some-times the nurse fed ba-by out of a bot-tle. If ba-by left some of his food, nurse gave it to his sis-ters, for they li-ked his food bet-ter than their own sup-pers.

Jes-sy beg-ged nurse to let her be the ba-by's maid. So the nurse sent Jes-sy to fetch what-ever ba-by want-ed. Jes-sy did not care for the trou-ble. She li-ked to run a-bout for ba-by. She lov-ed him bet-ter than all her toys.

Ad-am and Eve had two sons. Their names were Cain and A-bel. Cain was wick-ed. He ha-ted his broth-er A-bel A-bel did not hate Cain. A-bel lov-ed God, and he lov-ed his broth-er.

Cain ha-ted A-bel more and more.

One day he was a-lone with A-bel a-mong the green hills and the green trees, when he gave him a great blow, and kill-ed him.

Cain did not think that God saw him, but God did see him, and He was an-gry with Cain.

God said, "Where is your broth-er A-bel?"

Cain re-plied, "I do not know."

That was not true. Cain was a li-ar as well as a mur-der-er. He was like Sa-tan.

God told Cain that He had seen his broth-er's blood on the ground. He told Cain to go far a-way.

Cain was a-fraid that some one might kill him. But God set a mark up-on Cain, and He said, " If any one kills you I shall pun-ish him."

So no one kill-ed Cain.

Cain went far a-way from God and from his home.

He had some chil-dren. Cain's chil-dren were wick-ed. They did not love God, or wish to please Him.

Cain built a town. Cain's chil-dren liv-ed in it; so it was Sa-tan's town, be-cause Sa-tan is the fath-er of the wick-ed.

Ad-am and Eve had an-oth-er son. They gave him the name of Seth. He was sent to be a com-fort. Seth was like A-bel. He taught his chil-dren to pray to God.

word	work	ur
worth	work-man	la-bour
world	work-shop	fa-vour
worse	work-house	par-lour
worst	wor-ship	col-our

Worm

Tell the Child that or *is sometimes sounded* ur.

Kate went to see A-my. A-my said, "Do come and see my silk-worms."

They went in-to the par-lour.

There was a pa-per tray up-on a lit-tle ta-ble. There were green leaves in the pa-per tray. A-mong the leaves were lit-tle worms nib-bling the leaves with their lit-tle mouths.

Kate was quite sur-pris-ed to see them eat so much, for they were not big-ger than lit-tle pins.

"Are those worms of any use?" said she

"O yes! They do a great deal of work."

"What!" said Kate, "can worms work?

" Yes, they can spin silk," said A-my.

Kate said, " Pray show me some."

A-my said, " I have none yet; but I hope I shall have some soon."

So Kate went a-way that day.

In a month Kate came a-gain. She said to A-my, " Have the worms spun some silk ?"

" O yes," said A-my. " See this fine silk. Here is a skein of straw col-our, and here is an-other of lem-on col-our."

" But where are the silk-worms ?" said Kate.

" Here they are," said A-my, " in this lit-tle box, hid-den in the bran."

Kate found some ug-ly brown things in the bran. They were the worms turn-ed in-to grubs.

Kate came a-gain an-oth-er day. She said, " Where are the grubs ?" A-my show-ed her some crea-tures with wings like but-ter-flies " These were my grubs," said she.

Noah's Ark.

A long while a-go God said, "I will send much rain, and I will drown the peo-ple in the world by a flood"

But God said to No-ah, "I will save you and your fam-i-ly. Build an ark, and bring some beasts and some birds in-to the ark, and get a great deal of food and store it up in the ark."

So No-ah built an ark. While he was build-ing it—the wick-ed peo-ple went on in sin, and be-came worse and worse.

No-ah went in-to the ark with his wife,

and his three sons, and his sons' wives, and the beasts and the birds.

God shut the door when they were in. So none of the wick-ed peo-ple were a-ble to get in. The rain came, and drown-ed the world.

Once No-ah let a ra-ven go out of the win-dow; but the ra-ven came back no more.

Then No-ah sent a dear lit-tle dove, and the dove soon came back to the win-dow, and No-ah let her in.

Soon he sent the dove out a-gain, and she came back with a leaf in her beak.

No-ah soon sent her out a-gain, and she came back no more.

No-ah wait-ed till God bade him go out of the ark. When God spoke he came out, and he found the world was dry. He thank-ed God for sav-ing him.

He had been in the ark twelve months.

NOTE. — *Some words are not sounded as they are spelt,—*

have	*is sounded*	hav	said	*is sounded*	sed
are	„	ar	any	„	enny
were	„	wer	many	„	menny
			great	„	grate

Many chil-dren have been kill-ed by play-ing with gun-pow-der.

Mis-ter Ben-son kept a shop, and sold oil, can-dles, and many oth-er things.

One thing he sold was gun-pow-der.

A per-son came in and said, " Have you any gun-pow-der? I want to shoot birds."

Mis-ter Ben-son went to his can-is-ter for the gun-pow-der; but there was not any. A great boy was stand-ing near. It was Mis-ter Ben-son's son. Mis-ter Ben-son said to him, " Go up-stairs in-to the store-room and fill this can-is-ter with gun-pow-der."

The great boy went up-stairs and fill-ed the can-is-ter. Then it came in-to his fool-ish mind, " I will go in-to the nur-se-ry and fright-en my lit-tle broth-ers and sis-ters."

He had play-ed many tricks, and now he play-ed an-other trick. He throws a lit-tle gun-pow-der in-to the fire. And what hap-pens? The flames dart out and catch the pow-der in the can-is-ter. It is blown up with a loud noise. The chil-dren are thrown down,—they are in flames,—the win-dows are bro-ken—the house is sha-ken !

Mis-ter Ben-son hears the noise, and rush-es up-stairs. What a sight ! His chil-dren ly-ing on the floor burn-ing ! The ser-vants help to quench the flames. They go for a cab to take the chil-dren to the hos-pi-tal. The doc-tor says, " The chil-dren are blind, and they will soon die." And they died.

Long be-fore this world was made, the Son of God liv-ed a-bove the sky with God his Fa-ther. His Fa-ther told him to go down in-to this world to die for us—be-cause Ad-am and Eve had sin-ned, and we were all sin-ners.

So Je-sus came down from the sky to be a man, and to die. But first he was a lit-tle ba-by. His moth-er was poor. She had to make a long jour-ney. At night she stop-ped at an Inn to sleep. But the man at the Inn told her he had no room for her in the house, and he bade her go to the sta-ble. So she went in-to the sta-ble with the cows.

While she was in the sta-ble God sent her a ba-by. He was the Son of God. Yet he was weak like oth-er babes. His moth-er wrap-ped him up in long clothes. But he had no cra-dle; nothing but the hay and the straw to lie up-on.

While he was ly-ing near his moth-er, some men came to the door. God had told them of the Babe, while they were watch-ing the sheep on the hills. They came to see the Babe. They bow-ed down and wor-ship-ped him. They lov-ed that Babe, be-cause he was the Son of God. They went a-way, and they told e-ve-ry body they met—a-bout the Babe in the sta-ble.

What name did his moth-er give him?

She gave him the name of Je-sus.

Je-sus had no sin like oth-er babes. He nev-er did any-thing wrong. He o-bey-ed his moth-er. He came when she told him to come, and he went when she told him to go, and he stay-ed at home when she told him to stay.

NOTE.—*Let the Child be told that* oo *is not always long as in* moon *and* boot, *but that sometimes it is short, as in* foot.

Foot	good	book	look
soot	hood	rook	hook
wool	stood	took	shook

The Bi-ble is the best book in the world. It is the book of God. God told good men what to write. The Bi-ble tells us a-bout Je-sus. When Je-sus liv-ed in this world he did good to poor sick peo-ple. He took a blind man by the hand, and led him out of the town, and touch-ed his eyes, and made him look up and see. He stood by the bed of a lit-tle girl who had just di-ed, he took her hand and said, "Rise up," and she got up and felt quite well.

Once some moth-ers led some dear lit-tle ones to the Lord Je-sus. Some men were so un-kind as to want to send the chil-dren a-way. They said it would be a trouble to Je-sus to have chil-dren come to Him.

But Je-sus did not think chil-dren trouble-some. He lov-ed the lit-tle ones. He said to the un-kind men, " Let the lit-tle chil-dren come un-to me." What sweet words! See, He takes them in His arms and bless-es them! What hap-py lit-tle crea-tures! They like sit-ting up-on His knee, and look-ing at Him as He smiles up-on them.

Does Je-sus love chil-dren? O yes, they are His own lambs, His own doves—His lit-tle sons and daugh-ters. He came down from a-bove to save the lit-tle ones, as well as the grown-up peo-ple. There are a great many lit-tle chil-dren with Him now a-bove the sky.

Pud-ding	pul-pit	care-ful
put	but-cher	spite-ful
puss	cush-i-on	hate-ful
push	joy-ful	grate-ful
bush	pain-ful	sloth-ful
full	use-ful	du-ti-ful
pull	play-ful	beau-ti-ful
bull		

Lit-tle Er-nest was at din-ner one day. He look-ed and saw a rich plum pud-ding on the ta-ble. He wish-ed for some. He saw a plain pud-ding, too; but he did not wish for that. His Mam-ma gave him some plain pud-ding, be-cause it was good for him, but he push-ed a-way his plate and said, "I do not want that." Then his Mam-ma said, "You cannot have plum pud-ding, it would not be good for you."

Then Er-nie pout-ed and frown-ed.

He said, "I will have no din-ner." Was not that naugh-ty? So his Mam-ma let him go with-out his din-ner. Poor child! How much he want-ed his tea by tea-time! He was but a lit-tle child, he was on-ly three years old when he be-ha-ved in this naugh-ty man-ner. Next day he did not push a-way his plate, but he took what-ev-er his Mam-ma gave him.

An-oth-er lit-tle boy, na-med Ar-thur, want-ed some-thing on the ta-ble, and his Mam-ma said "No." He could not help cry-ing, for he was on-ly two years old, but he hid his tears in his nurse's a-pron, and wi-ped them a-way soon, and he took what his Mam-ma gave him.

He tried to look pleas-ed, and he said, " *That* not good for me." " No, dar-ling," said his Mam-ma, "that would make you ill."

1 *is silent in these word*

Wolf

wo-man	could
wo-men	would
worst-ed	sh ould

wolves

Fan-ny was a lit-tle girl, who liv-ed in a coun-try far a-way o-ver the sea.

She liv-ed in a far-m up-on a gr-een com-mon. By the side of the com-mon there was a great wood; but Fan-ny nev-er ran in-to the wood, be-cause there were wolves in the wood. In our coun-try there are no wolves, but in Fan-ny's coun-try there were many wolves.

Fan-ny had a lit-tle broth-er, nam-ed Mar-tin. She lov-ed this lit-tle broth-er very much.

Fan-ny's Mam-ma died when Mar-tin was a ba-by. When Mar-tin was five, and Fan-ny was twelve, Pa-pa died too. When he was dy-ing, he said to Fan-ny, "Take care of your lit-tle broth-er. Be a moth-er to him."

Fan-ny nev-er for-got what her Pa-pa said as he was dy-ing. She took great care of her lit-tle broth-er.

She had to work hard to get food. She pick-ed up wool on the com-mon. There were sheep feed-ing there, and much wool drop-ped from their backs. Lit-tle Mar-tin help-ed Fan-ny to pick up the wool. They fill-ed many bags with wool.

Fan-ny took home the wool. She wash-ed it clean. Then she spun it on her spin-ning-wheel, and made the wool in-to worst-ed. Then she knit-ted the worst-ed into stock-ings.

When she had knit-ted a great many pairs, she took them to the town to sell them. She got many shil-lings from the peo-ple of the town. She went to a shop with the shil-lings, and got food for her-self and her broth-er.

Who took care of Mar-tin while Fan-ny was in the town?

A good old wo-man came to live with Fan-ny in her cot, and she took care of Mar-tin when Fan-ny was out.

Mar-tin did not go to school, for there was no school near the cot. So Fan-ny took pains to teach him to read.

She show-ed him how to knit wool and to plat straw. But she let him play most of the day on the com-mon. She told him nev-er to go out of her sight, and nev-er to go in-to the wood, be-cause of the wolves. So Mar-tin gath-er-ed wild flow-ers on the com-mon, or else pick-ed up wool to bring home to Fan-ny.

For two years Fan-ny and Mar-tin and the old wo-man liv-ed hap-pi-ly to-ge-ther in the cot. Fan-ny was now four-teen and Mar-tin was sev-en.

It was win-ter. The ground was quite cov-er-ed with snow. The wolves had nothing to eat. They were so hun-gry that they left the wood, and prowl-ed about the com-mon. A pack of wolves went to-ge-ther. It made peo-ple trem-ble to hear the howl-ing of the wolves at night. Fan-ny tri-ed to keep her door shut night and day.

But one day the door was left o-pen. Fan-ny was ba-king some loaves she had made. Wolves like the smell of hot loaves. Fan-ny was ta-king her loaves out of the o-ven, when some wolves smell-ed them.

Fan-ny look-ed up and saw a wolf com-ing in at the door. Lit-tle Mar-tin was play-ing a-bout, and the old woman was knit-ting in the cor-ner. Fan-ny snatch-ed up a great

 stick. She was just
go-ing to kill the
wolf with the stick,
when an-oth-er wolf
rush-ed in and ran
up to lit-tle Mar-tin.
Fan-ny saw him. She
let go her stick, push-ed her broth-er in-to a
cup-board, and lock-ed him in.

While Fan-ny was do-ing this, the first
wolf sprang up-on Fan-ny, seiz-ed her by the
throat, and cho-ked her in a mo-ment.

And what be-came of the old wo-man?

She tried to save Fan-ny; but she could
not, for the wolves tore her flesh off her bones
very quick-ly.

But they could not get at lit-tle Mar-tin. He
was safe in the cup-board. He heard the wolves
eat-ing up his sis-ter and the old wo-man.

When the wolves had done eating their flesh, they did not stop to eat the loaves, but went back to their dens in the wood.

Mar-tin was still in the cup-board; for he could not get out, as the door was lock-ed.

But a neigh-bour saw the wolves com-ing out of the cot. She came in, and saw the floor cov-er-ed with blood and bones, and heard Mar-tin scream-ing in the cup-board. She un-lock-ed the door, and let lit-tle Mar-tin out.

How he wept to think that his sis-ter had been eat-en up by the wolves! Oh, how much he lov-ed her for giv-ing up her life to save his!

Was she not like the Lord Je-sus, who died that we might live for ev-er. He sav-ed us from that worst of wolves—Sa-tan; who hates men, and tries to destroy them.

NOTE.— *Tell the Child that* a *sometimes has a broad sound, as in* Mamma.

	ast	ask	ant
Glass	last	task	can't
ass	mast	bask	shan't
pass	past	flask	grant
brass	cast		slant
class	fast	ath	
a-las		path	asp
	aff	bath	clasp
bas-ket	staff	fath-er	anch
mas-ter	af-ter	rath-er	branch

A shep-herd took his lit-tle boy with him to the moun-tains. The lit-tle fel-low was on-ly three years old. He was much pleas-ed to go with his fath-er. The shep-herd took his dog to help him take care of his sheep.

The fath-er and his boy went up and down the green hills for a long while

At last the lit-tle child was rath-er tir-ed. So the kind fath-er said to him, "Stop here, my dar-ling, with the dog, while I go up yon-der hill to look after the sheep. I will soon come back."

So the lit-tle boy stay-ed with the dog.

The shep-herd climb-ed a-lone to the top of the high hill. Just as he was look-ing a-round, the sky be-came dark and a fog cov-er-ed the hills. The shep-herd went down the hill as fast as he could, but he did not go by the right path, for it was so dark he could not find it.

He reach-ed his home that night with-out his child or his dog. A-las! a-las! how sad were the fath-er and moth-er that night with-out their lit-tle dar-ling! The broth-ers and sis-ters ask-ed their fath-er af-ter the lit-tle one; but he could only an-swer, "God grant that we may find him soon."

The next day the shep-herd set out with his neigh-bours to look for the child.

Af-ter the fath-er had left home the dog came run-ning up the path. He seem-ed hun-gry, so the moth-er gave him a bit of oat-cake. He took it in his mouth and ran a-way.

At night the shep-herd re-turn-ed. "Alas!" said he, "I have not found my child!" He was much cast down that night, and could hard-ly sleep for fret-ting.

Next day he set a-bout his sad task a-gain, and he spent the day look-ing for his boy.

Af-ter he had left home — the dog came a-gain to ask, in his way, for his food. A-gain he did not eat his cake, but trot-ted a-way with it.

When the shep-herd came home, he was told a-bout the dog. So he did not leave home the next day, but wait-ed for the dog

Soon the dog came and got his bit of cake. This time his mas-ter went af-ter him.

The dog led the way up a moun-tain path; then the dog went down a slant-ing path, o-ver a stream, in-to a cave.

The shep-herd, by the help of his staff, got down in-to this cave.

His joy was great when he saw his child sit-ting in the cave eat-ing the cake, and the dog ly-ing near, look-ing at his lit-tle mas-ter.

The shep-herd clasp-ed his boy in his arms, and then he clasp-ed his faith-ful dog to his heart.

The child had wan-der-ed in the dark to this cave, and had been a-fraid to go o-ver the stream : so the dog had fed him day by day with his own cake. By night and by day the dog had watch-ed by the side of the child.

Who would not love such a dog ?

NOTE.— *The following words have the broad sound of* a. *and* laugh *like* laff.

half	calm	castle
calf	balm	branch
half	palm	an-swer
laugh	psalm	com-mand

Aunt
jaunt

A good moth-er used to teach her chil-dren lit-tle vers-es out of the Bi-ble. She had two lit-tle girls, named Het-ty and Mil-ly. One day the moth-er taught them this verse—

" The dark-ness hi-deth not from Thee."

This is a verse of a psalm.

The moth-er told the chil-dren that God could see them in the dark as well as in the light

" Can God see me when I am in the house ?" ask-ed Mil-ly.

"Yes," re-plied Mam-ma; " He can see you when the door is shut and when the blinds are down."

Mil-ly seem-ed rath-er sad, for she did many naugh-ty things when her Mam-ma was out of the room.

The two girls, Het-ty and Mil-ly, used to go to school in the day and to come back at night.

One morn-ing as Mil-ly was put-ting on her bon-net to go to school, she could not find her gloves. So she ran in-to the par-lour to look for them.

On the ta-ble there was a bas-ket full of bits of plum-cake. It was a pres-ent from Aunt Fanny to Mil-ly's Mam-ma.

Mil-ly was fond of plum-cake; but it was her moth-er's com-mand that she should nev-er touch it with-out leave.

She did not for-get the com-mand; but she want-ed to taste the cake. So she snatch-ed up a great bit of cake and put it in her pock-et.

At this mo-ment she re-mem-ber-ed the words of the psalm —

" The dark-ness hi-deth not from Thee."

But she did not think God saw her at that mo-ment. She was not a-fraid of God. She was on-ly a-fraid of her moth er, and her moth-er was up-stairs.

Mil-ly ran to school.

As she was run-ning she met two girls. She said to them, " Oh, you don't know what I've got! Look in here!"

So they look-ed in-to her poc-ket and said, " Oh! did your moth-er give you such a big bit?"

Mil-ly did not an-swer.

Just then Het-ty came run-ning up.

Mil-ly said to the two girls. " Don't tell ! I don't want Het-ty to know what I've got !"

Then she whis-per-ed to the girls, " I will give you half the cake."

The teach-er rang a bell at the school-door. The girls went in-to the school-room.

Mil-ly did not be-have well in the class. She did not mind her les-sons, but laugh-ed and whis-per-ed with the oth-er girls. She was un-easy in her mind, and could not be qui-et.

Het-ty was calm and good, and did her les-sons right

At din-ner time Milly went in-to the gar-den and hid her-self be-hind the thick branch-es of a tree.

Two girls fol-low-ed her and ask-ed her

M

for half the cake. They did not know that Mil-ly had sto-len the cake. They ask-ed her man-y times how she got it, but Mil-ly would not an-swer.

In the even-ing Het-ty and Mil-ly re-turn-ed home.

When the maid un-dress-ed Mil-ly, she said, "What have you had in your poc-ket to grease your dress?"

"Noth-ing," said Mil-ly.

That was a lie.

As soon as Mil-ly was in bed she re-mem-ber-ed the words of the psalm,—

"The dark-ness hi-deth not from Thee."

"A-las!" said Mil-ly to her-self, "God sees me now. He has seen me in the day, and now He sees me at night. I have sto-len and told lies. What will be-come of me!"

Mil-ly began to cry and to sob.

The maid was in the room fold-ing up Mil-ly's clothes. She saw some-thing was the mat-ter, so she went and fetch-ed her mis-tress.

When the kind moth-er came, she went close up to Mil-ly's bed and said, "What is the mat-ter, my child?"

Then Mil-ly with many tears told her moth-er what she had done.

The moth-er an-swer-ed,—"Con-fess your sin to God, my child, and He will for-give you, and wash a-way your guilt in the blood of Je-sus."

Then the moth-er knelt down and pray-ed for Mil-ly, while Mil-ly knelt up in her bed.

When the moth-er went a-way, Mil-ly pray-ed to God a-lone, and shed many more tears.

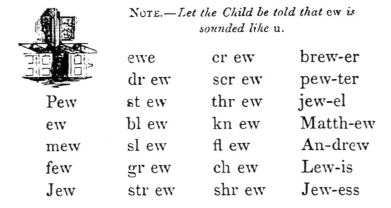

NOTE.—*Let the Child be told that* ew *is sounded like* u.

	ewe	cr ew	brew-er
	dr ew	scr ew	pew-ter
Pew	st ew	thr ew	jew-el
ew	bl ew	kn ew	Matth-ew
mew	sl ew	fl ew	An-drew
few	gr ew	ch ew	Lew-is
Jew	str ew	shr ew	Jew-ess

E-dith was a child who pit-ied the poor, the sick, and the rag-ged. One day, when she was on-ly three years old, she was stand-ing by her Mam-ma. Her Mam-ma was speak-ing to a poor wo-man. The poor wo-man held a lit-tle child by the hand. E-dith knew the child was cold, for the wind blew hard. She took her own shawl and threw it o-ver the child.

E-dith went with her Aunt to stay in the

coun-try. She went to see poor peo-ple. One day the Aunt ask-ed E-dith wheth-er she would like to make some clothes for a poor child. E-dith an-swer-ed, "Yes, please, Aunt, I should like it so much."

So her Aunt said, "For what poor child would you rath-er make some-thing?"

"Oh, Aunt!" cried E-dith, "I saw a poor, weak, lit-tle babe in its moth-er's arms, such a dear, sick, lit-tle thing. I should so like to make it a frock."

"Well," an-swer-ed her Aunt, "you shall make it a frock."

In the after-noon E-dith went out with her Aunt to a shop. She chose some pink cot-ton print. She ask-ed her Aunt to cut out a long frock. So her Aunt cut out a long frock. E-dith made it in a few days, and then took it her-self to the poor babe.

A long while a-go the Lord Je-sus liv-ed in this world.

He was born in the land of the Jews. His moth-er was a Jew-ess.

She was a good wo-man.

God was the Fath-er of the Lord Je-sus.

When Je-sus grew up to be a man, He went a-bout preach-ing.

A few friends went a-bout with Him.

One of them was na-med An-drew.

One of them was na-med Mat-thew.

One day Je-sus was in a ship on the sea. His twelve friends were with Him. The wind blew hard and the waves rose high. Jesus said to the winds and waves, " Be still."

Then there was a great calm.

One day there was a great crowd of peo-ple fol-low-ing Je-sus   At last the peō-ple grew hun-gry.   Je-sus had a few loaves and fish-es He said to His friends, " We will feed the peo-ple."   The friends said, " How can we feed so many peo-ple with a few loaves and fish-es ? "

But Je-sus made the peo-ple sit down, and His friends fed them with the five loaves and the two fishes.

And the peo-ple had as much as they could eat, and they threw down lit-tle bits up-on the ground.

Je-sus knew that He must be kill-ed.   At last Je-sus told His friends that He soon should die.   He sent them to fetch an ass for Him to ride up-on in-to the town.   Many peō-ple came to meet Him.   They pluck-ed branch-es of palm and strew-ed them in the way.   Lit-tle chil-dren sang His praise as they saw Him pass.

NOTE.—*Let the Child be taught the sounds of all these* diphthongs, *already learned separately. Let them be read downwards,* not *across, at first.*

ai	ea	oa	ui	ei	ey	ew
a	e	o	u	a	a	u
wait	beat	coat	fruit	veil	they	pew
bait	meat	boat	suit	weigh	prey	few

au	aw	ou	ow	oy	oi	oo
fault	claw	loud	cow	boy	boil	moon
cause	draw	proud	how	joy	spoil	spoon

Bil-ly was a sil-ly lit-tle boy. He could not un-der-stand as well as most chil-dren. He could not work for his liv-ing like many boys. He had a sis-ter who was a maid in a rich fam-i-ly, and she gave some of her mon-ey to Bil-ly and his fath-er and moth-er. Bil-ly was al-low-ed to go and see his sis-ter in the grand house when-ev-er he pleas-ed.

One day, as he was go-ing to see his sis-ter,

he saw some-thing bright shin-ing in the grass
He pick-ed it up, and he saw it was a beau-ti-ful
sil-ver spoon, such as he had nev-er seen be-fore.
He knew that if he were to sell it he should get
much mon-ey for it. But he knew that God
had said, "Thou shalt not steal." He put the
spoon up his coat-sleeve to hide it, and he
went to the great house.

He told the ser-vants he must see the la-dy.
He was shown in-to the draw-ing-room, which
was full of com-pany. He ap-proach-ed the
la-dy, pull-ed the spoon out of his sleeve, and
gave it to the la-dy, say-ing, "Thou shalt not
steal." He went on say-ing, a-loud, "Thou
shalt not steal." The la-dy ask-ed him where
he found the spoon. Bil-ly re-plied, "Under
the kitch-en win-dow—Bil-ly found—" "Thou
shalt not steal."*

* "Early Days," *a Penny Periodical.*

Bread	ef	es
ed	deaf	pl eas-ant
dead	et	el
head	thr eat	jeal-ous
dr ead	ent	eth (*hard*)
tr ead	meant	leath-er
th read	eth	feath-er
sp read	death	weath-er
read-y	ev	ek
in-stead	heav-en	break-fast

One day Lau-ra hurt her foot. How did she hurt it? Lau-ra was wil-ful in the nurs-e-ry. Sal-ly said, "I am read-y to dress you." But Lau-ra was ri-ding on the rock-ing horse. She would go on ri-ding. She would

not mind Sal-ly. Sal-ly pull-ed Lau-ra. Lau-ra
spread out her arms, and clung round the head
and neck of the horse. Sal-ly pull-ed more and
more. At last—down came Lau-ra, and the
wood-en horse too. The horse was heav-y.
The weight crush-ed Lau-ra's lit-tle foot.
Lau-ra scream-ed in a dread-ful man-ner.
Lau-ra's mother rush-ed up-stairs. She was
a-fraid that one of her chil-dren was dead.
" What is the mat-ter ?" cried Mam-ma, quite
out of breath. She was glad to find that no
one was dead. Mam-ma said, " Fetch a bot-tle
of bran-dy." Nurse put a lit-tle bran-dy in
a ba-sin Nurse ba-thed Lau-ra's foot in the
bran-dy. At last the child be-came quiet
Mam-ma did not pun-ish Lau-ra for her naugh-
ti-ness, be-cause her foot was hurt. Lau-ra
was not able to tread up-on the ground for
a month.

Note.—*Let the Child be told that* ear *is some-
times sounded as* er.

	earn	erch	earth
Pearl	learn	search	earth-quake
erl	erd	erse	earth-worm
earl-y	heard	hearse	earth-en-ware

Pearls are beau-ti-ful white stones. Pearls are not found in the earth. I have heard that they are found in oys-ter shells at the bot-tom of the sea. Men go down to search for them. A man who search-es for oys-ters is let down from a ship, by a rope. He holds a bas-ket in one hand. It is dark at the bot-tom of the sea : the man stretch-es out one arm, and feels for the oys-ters. He can-not stop long, be-cause his breath is stop-ped, and he would soon die. So he pulls the rope, and men pull him up. In this way the man earns his bread.

Ro-sa found a dead bird ly-ing on the earth in the gar-den. It was a Ro-bin Red-breast. It had red feath-ers on its breast.

Ro-sa pick-ed up the bird, and took it home. She laid it in a draw-er in the nurs-e-ry. She meant to get some hay, and to make a nest for her bird; and she meant to get some white stones, and to lay them in the nest in-stead of eggs.

She told her Mam-ma a-bout the bird. Her Mam-ma said, "My dear child, you can-not keep your bird."

"Why not, Mam-ma?"

"Be-cause it will soon de-cay, and be eat-en by worms."

"O Mam-ma! I nev-er heard that be-fore. I will not keep my bird."

So Ro-sa flew up-stairs, and threw the dead bird out of the nurs-e-ry win-dow.

Ce-dar

Ci-der

Cy-press

NOTE.—*Tell the Child that c when it comes before e, i, or y has the sound of s.*

ce	ci	cy
ceil-ing	cin-der	cym-bal
re-ceive	cit-y	mer-cy
de-ceive	civ-il	Lu-cy
cell	cir-cle	Per-cy
cel-lar	pen-cil	Per-ci-val
cer-tain	dis-ci-ple	Cyp-ri-an
gro-cer	ac-ci-dent	ac-cept
sau-cer	cru-ci-fy	ex-cept
Fran-ces	Fran-cis	ex-ceed

Ce-li-a was ten years old. She had a lit-tle ta-ble of her own. It was cov-er-ed with pret-ty things she had re-ceiv-ed from her friends.

There was a glass deer and an i-vo-ry ship, and a wax ba-by in a chi-na cra-dle, and a ti-ny tea-pot, with a cir-cle of cups and sau-cers on a paint-ed tray, and many oth-er toys on the ta-ble.

Ce-li-a had a lit-tle sis-ter who could just run a-lone. Her name was Lu-cy. One day Lu-cy came to look at the toys, but she was so short that she could hard-ly see them; so she stood on tip-toe, and leant her hands a-gainst the ta-ble. She leant too hard.

The ta-ble was up-set. The toys fell up-on the floor. Many of the toys were bro-ken.

What did Ce-li-a say when she heard of this?

She said, " Poor little Lu-cy! She could not help up-set-ting the table. It was an ac-ci-dent. She was good not to touch the toys."

Was not Ce-li-a kind and mer-ci-ful?

Je-sus knew He was soon go-ing to be cru-ci-fied. He had twelve disciples. They were His friends. He said to them, " I will eat sup-per with you be-fore I die."

He took bread and broke it, and gave it to His dis-ci-ples, and He said, " This is my bod-y, which is bro-ken for you."

And He pour-ed wine in-to a cup, and gave it to his dis-ci-ples to drink, and He said, " This is my blood, shed for you and for many."

Then He left the room, and went to a gar-den. His dis-ci-ples came with Him to the gar-den.

Je-sus told them to pray, and then He went by Him-self to pray to His Father.

He was in great pain, and blood came out of His skin, and fell in big drops up-on the ground.

His dis-ci-ples fell a-sleep while Je-sus was pray-ing. When He had done pray-ing, He woke His dis-ci-ples, and said, "Rise up and let us go."

Sud-den-ly a number of men were seen com-ing near. They were wick-ed men who hat-ed Je-sus. They had staves or sticks in their hands. It was dark, but the wick-ed men had lamps.

A man na-med Ju-das came up and kiss-ed Je-sus. Ju-das was one of the dis-ci-ples; but he was wick-ed, and did not love Je-sus. He pre-tend-ed to love Him: but he could not de-ceive Je-sus.

Je-sus said to him, "Friend, why do you kiss me?"

The wick-ed men seiz-ed hold of Je-sus, and bound His hands, and led Him a-way, like a lamb to the slaugh-ter.

NOTE.—*In the following words the Child is taught the soft sound of c in syllables ending with ce and ces.*

	eece	ice	nce
Face	fleece	nice	juice
ace	peace	rice	oi
pace	piece	mice	oice
lace	niece	slice	voice
place		spice	oun
grace		twice	ounce
dis-grace		thrice	bounce

la-ces	pie-ces	spi-ces	jui-ces
fa-ces	nie-ces	sli-ces	voi-ces

ance	ence	ince	unce
dance	pence	mince	dunce
lance	fence	prince	won
prance	ab-sence	quince	one
France	si-lence	prin-ces	once

Sal-ly liv-ed with her great-grand-mo-ther. She lov-ed her Gran-ny much. Gran-ny was too old to work hard, and earn much mo-ney ; so she was poor. She was deaf, and nearly blind. She lov-ed Sal-ly more than any-thing on earth. She was her pet and her pearl.

A kind la-dy said to Gran-ny, " I will put Sal-ly to school. She will have plen-ty to eat, and she will learn to read and write."

The old wo-man thank-ed the kind la-dy, and said, " Sal-ly shall go where you please."

Sal-ly rose ear-ly one morn-ing to get read-y to go to school. She sat at break-fast with Gran-ny for the last time. Gran-ny cried much at part-ing with the dear lit-tle thing. She want-ed to give her some-thing as a keep-sake, but she had nothing to give her. At last she search-ed her pock-et, and found one far-thing and an old bro-ken key. She gave these to

Sally at School.

Sal-ly with ma-ny tears. Sal-ly cri-ed too. She kiss-ed her Gran-ny, and got in-to a cart to go to Lon-don. She came to a high house in a street. A neat little girl o-pen-ed the door. Sal-ly got out of the cart. A kind woman beg-ged her to come in. The woman was the mis-tress of the school.

Sal-ly had a sick-ly face. She had no col-our on her cheeks. She was thin and weak. Why was she ill? Be-cause Gran-ny had giv-en her too lit-tle food. Gran-ny could not af-ford to pay the price of meat or milk, for she had on-ly a few pence. So Sal-ly was half starved. But now she was come to school she had plen-ty of nice and whole-some food.

Lit-tle Sal-ly was good, and took pains to learn. She was not a dunce. She did not get into dis-grace. One day the mis-tress saw her with tears on her face. She said to her,

"What are you cry-ing a-bout?"

"A-bout my Gran-ny," she said. "I used to thread her nee-dles. I can-not tell what she will do with-out me, for she can-not see to thread her nee-dles." So the mis-tress said, "Pray to God, dear child, to com-fort your Gran-ny."

The child went in-to a cor-ner and pray-ed, "O God, pray bless my dear Gran-ny, and send some-body to thread her nee-dles for her. And when she dies, take her to Heav-en, and give her a crown of glory. Hear me, for Christ's sake. A-men."

Did God hear lit-tle Sal-ly? Yes. Kind peo-ple took care of her dear Gran-ny. And God gave her grace and peace.

NOTE. — *Teach the Child that g before e and i are sometimes soft like j; not always, for g is hard in get and give, and many other words.*

Gip-sy	gem	germ
gib-bet	gen-tle	Ger-man
gin	gen-tle-ness	ge-ra-ni-um
gin-ger	gen-tle-man	ges-ture
gin-ger-bread	gen-teel	Eu-gene
giant	gen-e-ral	cler-gy-man
gi-raffe	gen-e-rous	o-bli-ging
Giles	Gen-e-sis	en-gine

In sum-mer gip-sies wan-der from place to place, and sleep in tents. They do not know a-bout God. Some gip-sies have been taught by good peo-ple, and have turn-ed to God. But most gip-sies are ig-no-rant Some of them steal and tell lies.

Once a lit-tle boy, named Gill, went with his Mam-ma to a shop. It was a gro-cer's shop. While his Mam-ma was buy-ing some gin-ger cakes, lit-tle Gill stood at the door.

Soon his Mam-ma was ready to go. She look-ed for Gill; but she could not find him.

Mam-ma asked ev-e-ry one she met in the street, "Have you seen my lit-tle boy? He is four years old, and he is dress-ed in a blue frock and white trow-sers, and a straw hat."

At last a gen-tle-man said, "I have seen him."

"O where did you see him?" Mam-ma cri-ed out.

"I saw him with a gip-sy; but the gip-sy is sent to pris-on, and your lit-tle boy is safe."

Mam-ma found her boy in a house cry-ing. He said, "The gip-sy gave me gin-ger-bread, and ask-ed me to come with her." O what a sil-ly boy he was to go away with a gip-sy!

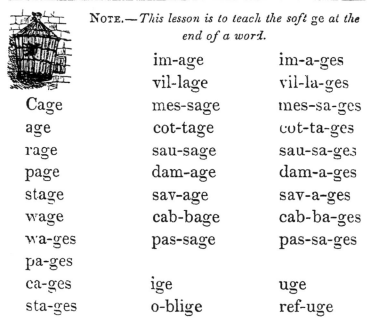

NOTE.—*This lesson is to teach the soft ge at the end of a word.*

	im-age	im-a-ges
	vil-lage	vil-la-ges
Cage	mes-sage	mes-sa-ges
age	cot-tage	cot-ta-ges
rage	sau-sage	sau-sa-ges
page	dam-age	dam-a-ges
stage	sav-age	sav-a-ges
wage	cab-bage	cab-ba-ges
wa-ges	pas-sage	pas-sa-ges
pa-ges		
ca-ges	ige	uge
sta-ges	o-blige	ref-uge

There is a great cit-y far a-way, where peo-ple wor-ship im-a-ges of wood and stone, and say they are gods. The peō-ple in that cit-y are near-ly black.

A kind, white la-dy tri-ed to teach them

a-bout the true God. One day she saw a poor wom-an ly-ing on the ground with a lit-tle boy by her side. The kind la-dy spoke to them; but the wom-an was too ill to an-swer her.

The lit-tle boy said, "My mother is sick and has nothing to eat, and I fear she will die."

The la-dy sent her ser-vant home with this mes-sage, "Let some men come to help a poor sick wom-an." Some men came and took the wom-an and the child to the la-dy's cot-tage. The mother and child were pla-ced on a nice clean mat with a blan-ket to cov-er them. But the mother died that night. Then the la-dy took care of the lit-tle boy. She found that he was proud of his name, be-cause it was the name of an im-age. His name was Ram-chun-der. But soon the boy wish-ed for a new name, and he was nam-ed John. Soon he lov-ed Je-sus and ha-ted im-a-ges.

adge	edge	idge	odge	udge
badge	hedge	ridge	lodge	judge
Madge	ledge	bridge	dodge	trudge
	sledge	midge	Hodge	grudge
arge	erge	irge	orge	urge
large	serge	dirge	gorge	surge
barge	verge		forge	scourge

An-drew was a brave, big lad. But he lik-ed to have his own way, and did not o-bey his moth-er.

He liv-ed near the sea.

One day a large ship came to that place. The cap-tain let An-drew come on board and look at the high masts, and the large sails. An-drew be-gan to wish to be a sail-or. The cap-tain said he would take him, if he li-ked to come. So An-drew went home to ask his moth-er's leave.

When he o-pen-ed the cot-tage door, he said to his moth-er, "Will you let me go to sea? I want to be a sailor."

"No," said his moth-er, "I can-not spare you: for you are my only son, and I am a wid-ow."

"And I can-not spare you," said lit-tle Madge; "for you are my on-ly broth-er, and you may be drown-ed at sea."

"No," ad-ded his moth-er. "No, An-drew! you must not go to sea!"

But An-drew did not o-bey his moth-er. One night he slip-ped down to the shore, and the next morn-ing he sail-ed a-way be-fore his moth-er was a-wake. When she a-woke and miss-ed her son, she wept, and so did Madge.

At first An-drew found it pleas-ant to sail in the ship. But soon a storm a-rose. The sur-ges dash-ed a-gainst the ship, and drove it a-gainst a sharp ledge of rock. The ship was bro-ken, and the waves rush-ed in. The sur-ges wash-ed a-way many of the men.

A few were left. An-drew was left.

It was now dark.

"What shall we do?" said the sail-ors "Can we get a-way in a boat?" said one.

"The boats are wash-ed a-way," said an-oth-er.

The sail-ors got some boards, and tied them to-geth-er with ropes, and so made a raft to float up-on the sea. An-drew got up-on the raft with the rest of the sail-ors.

The whole night long they were toss-ed up and down up-on the raft. When morn-ing came, An-drew found him-self a-lone. The sail-ors had been wash-ed a-way one by one.— But An-drew had clung fast, and God had kept him from death.

An-drew look-ed a-round up-on the great sea, and saw a long way off a white sail.

"Will the peo-ple in that ship see me?" said An-drew. He pray-ed to God to make them see him. God heard his pray-er. The ship's crew saw him, and sail-ed up to him.

Oh, what was his joy when he saw the ship com-ing!

The sail-ors lift-ed him on board, and laid him on a nice soft bed. Then he be-gan to con-fess his naugh-ti-ness in dis-o-bey-ing his moth-er. Then he pray-ed for mer-cy.

God let him get safe home to his moth-er's cot-tage. He threw him-self at his moth-er's feet, and beg-ged for-give-ness.

He stay-ed at home some time; but at last his moth-er gave him leave to go to sea again: and then he went. And he grew up to be a good man.*

* *Taken from* "Early Days."

An-gel

Note.—In these words the a is sounded long, and the ge is soft like j.

ange	dan-ger
change	man-ger
strange	strang-er
chan-ged	chang-ing

Look at the cat-er-pil-lar on that leaf. One day it will be chan-ged in-to a but-ter-fly.

Look at the pink blos-som on that tree. One day it will be changed in-to an ap-ple.

Look at that a-corn ly-ing on the ground Dig a hole for the a-corn and co-ver it up. One day the a-corn will be changed in-to a great oak-tree.

God can change e-ve-ry-thing by his great pow-er. He can change a dead body in-to a liv-ing body. When Je-sus comes a-gain in the clouds he will change dead peo-ple in-to liv-ing peo-ple.

When the wick-ed peo-ple led Je-sus a-way, they took him to the pal-ace of a rich man. The rich man and his friends hated Je-sus. They were glad to see him with his hands bound. They ask-ed him wheth-er he was the Son of God. Je-sus said he was the Son of God. Then the wick-ed men said he de-served to die.

When it was light they took him to the judge. The judge's name was Pi-late. The judge said that Je-sus look-ed good. Then the wick-ed men were more angry, and said,

"Cru-ci-fy him! cru-ci-fy him!"

Pi-late said, "Shall I cru-ci-fy your king?"

The peo-ple said, "We will not have him for our king."

Pi-late said, "I will scourge him and let him go."

"No," said the peo-ple, "cru-ci-fy him"

O how cru-el! how un-grate-ful!

NOTE.—*In these words* a *has the sound of* au.

	salt	war
	false	war-ble
Ball	bald	ward
all	scald	ward-robe
call	al-so	re-ward
wail	al-though	warm
fall	al-ways	wa-ter
hall	al-most	wa-ter-fall
small	wal-nut	swarm

In these words the l *is not sounded.*   dwarf

| talk | stalk | Os-wald |
| walk | chalk | Al-ban |

One day Pa-pa said, " Come here, Os-wald."
But Os-wald did not come. Then Pa-pa went
to Os-wald and said, " Look at these small balls.
I meant to give them all to you, but as you did
not come when I call-ed, I shall keep them all.

Os-wald look-ed vex-ed, and walk-ed a-way.

Ed-ward was a care-less boy. Did you ev-er hear how he scald-ed his legs? He had strong legs, and he trip-ped light-ly a-long; but one day he scald-ed his legs. I will tell you how it hap-pen-ed.

He was go-ing to bathe in a small room. There was a great tub of cold water in the room. Nurse brought up a can of hot water, that Ed-ward might have a warm bath. Nurse went to fetch a piece of flan-nel. While she was out of the room, Ed-ward took up the can and tri-ed to pour the water in-to the tub; but the can was too heavy and he let it fall, and the water scald-ed his feet and legs. Poor boy! how he did squall! Nurse came run-ning back to know what was the mat-ter. She put some white flour up-on his legs to make them well. But it was a long while be-fore Ed-ward could walk out of doors a-gain.

	broth	of-ten	ought
	cloth	sof-ten	nought
Cross	moth	off	sought
oss	gone	cough	fought
toss	broad	stor-y	bought
loss	cof-fin	glor-y	brought
lost	cof-fee	Dora	thought

I will tell you the story of a good and grateful dog. Wil-li-am, a boy of eight years old, was walk-ing in the streets one day. He saw a poor wretch-ed dir-ty dog. It look-ed as if it had been ill treated. This dog fol-low-ed the lit-tle boy. The poor dog was lame and came limp-ing af-ter the boy.

When Wil-li-am got to the door of his home, he did not know wheth er he might bring the dog in. So he called for his moth-er and said,

" I have brought home a dog. May I bring it in-to the house?"

The moth-er look-ed at the dog and pit-ied it, be-cause it was thin, sick, and lame ; but she thought it was too dir-ty for the house. She al-low-ed the dog to be brought in-to the wash-house. All the chil-dren came run-ning to see the dog. The dog seemed to know it might not come in-to the house, and it fix-ed its large brown eyes up-on the chil-dren. The chil-dren al-most cri-ed at its sad look. They ran to fetch food for it. They soon re-turned with a few bones and a dish of wa-ter. The dog ate and drank ea-ger-ly.

The next thing was to get a bed for the dog. The chil-dren sought for clean straw, and soon brought some in a large bas-ket. They hoped the dog's cough would get well from the warmth of this nice bed.

In a few days no one would have known the dog to be the same. It was chang-ed from an ug-ly, hun-gry, dir-ty dog in-to a clean, play-ful, and pret-ty dog.

It was also a thank-ful dog. It show-ed its thank-ful-ness by frisk-ing and jump-ing a-bout the chil-dren, and lick-ing their hands.

The chil-dren call-ed it Rose and made it their friend. A good friend Rose was to them.

There were four chil-dren, Wil-li-am, the boy of eight, was the eld-est. Al-ban was a boy of six. Grace was four years old. Dora, the young-est, was on-ly three

The four chil-dren went to school ev-e-ry day. Rose u-sed to go with them. Bad boys often came near the chil-dren and tried to tease and hurt them. Rose bark-ed at these bad boys and fright-en-ed them; so that they ran off.

There was a broad street to be cross-ed on the way to school. It is hard for chil-dren to cross a broad street. Carts and coach-es and wag-ons may roll o-ver them, and break their bones. Rose al-ways look-ed to see wheth-er any carts were com-ing a-long the street, and she bark-ed at the chil-dren to keep them back, un-til the carts were gone past.

When the chil-dren were safe in the school, then Rose ran home. But she was not i-dle at home. She stay-ed in the yard with the fowls and chick-ens. She watch-ed them that they did not stray, and that no bad boys threw stones at them.

In the e-ven-ing the moth-er of-ten said,

" Rose, it is time to fetch the chil-dren." Then Rose would set off to bring them home. At last Rose knew the right time, and would set off to school with-out the moth-er tell-ing her.

When it was wet, the moth-er gave the dog an um-brel-la for the chil-dren. Rose would hold the um-brel-la be-tween her teeth; nor would she ev-er let bad peo-ple take it from her; but she would hold it quite tight, and run past as fast as pos-si-ble.

LIZZIE'S LAST WORDS.

Let me tell you a-bout a lit-tle girl who had no good dog to take care of her when she went a-long the streets.

Liz-zie was five years old. She was able to read. She was fond of read-ing a-bout Je-sus.

When she heard that any one was dead, she oft-en ask-ed, " Is he gone to be with Je-sus?"

She had a broth-er na-med Wal-ter. He was six years old. He took great care of Liz-zie.

One day Wal-ter and Liz-zie went hand in hand to school. Af-ter school was o-ver, they set out hand in hand to re-turn home.

It was a storm-y, wind-y day. The rain beat in their fa-ces, so that they could hard-ly see their way. They came to a cor-ner, where they had to turn in-to an-oth-er street. As they were turn-ing, a fu-ne-ral pass-ed a-long. Liz-zie saw it, and call-ed out to Wal-ter, "Is some one gone to be with Je-sus?"

At that mo-ment a heav-y wag-on came by, and knock-ed down both the chil-dren. Wal-ter crawl-ed out from un-der the wag-on. But Liz-zie was crush-ed by the great wheel go-ing o-ver her lit-tle bod-y. She was ta-ken up dead, but her spirit was gone to be with Je-sus. Je-sus was the last word she spoke on earth.*

* "Lizzie's Last Day."--*Rogers, Pontefract.*

THE STORY OF THE CROSS.

The Jews ha-ted Je-sus and cri-ed out, "Cru-ci-fy him." So the judge, to please the Jews, let him be cru-ci-fied.

Je-sus had to bear his cross up-on his back. That cross was made of two large pie-ces of wood. It was too heavy for Je-sus to bear it all a-lone. A man was made to help him to bear it.

The judge sent his sol-diers to cru-ci-fy Je-sus. They laid the cross on the ground and Je-sus up-on it, and they stretched out his arms and they drove nails in-to his hands and fas-ten-ed them to the cross. They did the same to his feet. Then they lift-ed up the cross and stuck it in-to the earth. Je-sus was full of pain from his pier-ced hands and feet.

But he was not ang-ry with the wick-ed

men. He pray-ed to his Fa-ther to for-give them.

There were two thieves, each nail-ed to a cross, on each side of Je-sus. One of them pray-ed to Je-sus, and Je-sus for-gave that thief.

Many peo-ple cri-ed out. "Why does not Je-sus come down from the cross?" But Je-sus would not come down be-cause he chose to die for us that we might be saved.

At last Je-sus said, "I thirst."

A man dip-ped a sponge in vin-e-gar, and put it on a reed and gave it to Je-sus. Soon after this, Je-sus bowed his head and died.

God made the earth to shake when Je-sus died, and many peo-ple were fright-en-ed.

A sol-dier came and pier-ced his side, and blood and water flowed upon the ground.

NOTE.—*The letter a has the sound of* a *in* ai *in the following words.*

	Mary	hair-y	parents
Can-a-ry	dair-y	scarce	Clara
air-y	Fair-y	scarce-ly	Sarah

Mary often went into grand-mam-ma's room to see her can-a-ries. They lived in a large cage. There was hair, moss, and wool in the cage. One can-a-ry was a deep yel-low. He was call-ed Am-ber. The other was pale yel-low, and was call-ed Fai-ry. Mary saw Fai-ry build her nest. Fai-ry laid down the horse-hair first, and then the moss, and last of all the wool. The nest look-ed so pret-ty li-ned with soft white wool. Fai-ry laid three light green eggs in her nest. Then she sat in her nest, and hatch-ed the eggs. Mary was much pleased when the first lit-tle bird was seen.

THE YOUNG SAV-AGE.

A lit-tle hea-then boy liv-ed in a land far a-way, call-ed Aus-tra-lia. He had no fath-er nor moth-er. They were dead. He had two broth-ers a lit-tle old-er than him-self. The three boys wan-der-ed a-bout to-geth-er. They were sav-age boys. They had no cot-tage, not e-ven a hut. They slept in lit-tle tents made of boughs of trees. They knew how to make them. But they knew not God. They had nev-er heard of God. Yet they did not pray to an im-age. They had no God, no i-dol, no im-age. They nev-er pray-ed at all.

The big-ger boys could kill birds, but the lit-tle one could not. He stay-ed in the tent till his broth-ers came back with birds. Then the boys light-ed a fire and roast-ed the birds. The lit-tle one could grub up roots out of the

ground, and he ate them, as well as birds and eggs. But some-times he had no-thing to eat.

One day he saw some men cut-ting down trees. They said, "Come with us, and you shall see the white man's town." So the lit-tle sav-age went with the men. His broth-ers did not go with him.

At last the boy came to a town. He had nev-er seen a town, nor a vil-lage, nor a bridge, nor a cot-tage. He won-der-ed at the things he saw as he wan-der-ed a-bout the streets. But he had no bread to eat, nor place to lodge in. The wood-cut-ters had left him to take care of him-self. But God watch-ed over him.

The poor lit-tle sav-age was a stran-ger.

He knew no one. He had no friend. Some white chil-dren saw him. They pit-i-ed him. They took him to their cot-tage. They said, "Mother, do give this lit-tle stran-ger a piece of bread." Those chil-dren were kind. They were like angels to the lit-tle stranger. They sa-ved him from starv-ing. The mother gave him a piece of bread.

Then said the chil-dren, "He has no place to lodge in. Mother, do let him sleep here."

The Mother said, "I have no chamber for the lit-tle stran-ger; but he may lodge on the floor in the shop."

The sav-age was glad to sleep in such a nice place. What a change it was for him! for he had been us-ed to sleep on the damp cold earth. He wrap-ped him-self in his blan-ket and went to sleep. He could not thank God, for he knew him not.

Next day the good moth-er gave the stran-
ger a piece of bread for break-fast. The
chil-dren went to school. The lit-tle sav-age
went too. The school-room seem-ed a strange
place to him. He did not know what the
chil-dren were do-ing with the books and the
slates, but he sat still and made no noise.

While the little sav-age was at school—a
gen-tle-man came in. He saw the boy sit-ting
in a cor-ner. This gen-tle-man was a good cler-
gy-man. He went up to the lit-tle stranger,
and pat-ted his head, and spoke kind words to
him. The child felt much pleas-ed.

The white chil-dren went home and talk-ed
a-bout the cler-gy-man's kind-ness to the lit-tle
stran-ger. The wo-man walk-ed to the cler-
gy-man's house and said, " I am poor. Will
you give me money to buy bread, and meat,
and pud-ding, for the lit-tle stran-ger ?"

The cler-gy-man an-swer-ed, " Let him call at my house. I will give him food." He also bought cloth to make warm clothes for the boy.

Soon he said to the boy, "You may sleep here." But the boy slip-ped out at night and went back to the shop. Per-haps he lik-ed be-ing with those white chil-dren who were so kind to him at first. It seem-ed strange that he should like bet-ter to sleep on the floor than in a bed ; but he was a sav-age, and not us-ed to a bed.

One day the cler-gy-man said to the boy, "Will you go with me to Eng-land in a ship ? Will you go a-cross the wa-ter?" The boy thought he should like to go. He set sail. The ship was toss-ed by the waves, but the boy was not fright-en-ed. He was not a-fraid to climb the tall masts, for he was used to climb-ing trees. Once when he got to the top of the mast he said to the men, " Ver' near moon."

The young sav-age had no name when he first came; but now he was call-ed Wil-lie. He slept in a dark place at the foot of the stairs. He did not for-get to re-peat a lit-tle pray-er he had learn-ed at school. It was the Lord's Pray-er. "Our Fa-ther which art in hea-ven." He said this pray-er by him-self both night and morn-ing. He had no pa-rents on earth, but he had a Fa-ther in hea-ven.

When he first came to Eng-land he was shy. He li-ked to sit with his back to the com-pa-ny. But when he was told it was like a bear to do so, he did not turn his back any more.

He was much pleas-ed with the pret-ty things he saw in the shop win-dows.

When he saw any-thing he liked, he point-ed to it, and said, "Buy me that." He did not know it was wrong to want to have things.

He was fond of pic-tures. He liked best pic-tures of an-gels. As he look-ed at them he said, "Nice an-gels—nice face—ver' nice face."

He was also fond of ba-bies. There was one lit-tle ba-by that he would look at ev-e-ıy night as it lay a-sleep.

Some one ask-ed him why he was so fond of it.

Wil-lie said, "Ver' like an-gel."

But at last he fell ill. Eng-land was too cold. The cold made him ill Be-fore he was ill, God chang-ed his heart. Wil-lie was not self-ish now, but lov-ing and grate-ful.

As he was dy-ing, he said, "If Je-sus had not died, I should have gone to Sa-tan."

Wil-lie went to be with Christ and the an-gels in glory ever-last-ing.

NOTE.—*In these words the a is sounded short, as in* can, *and not broad as in* star.

Par-rot	ar-row	par-ish
car-rot	mar-row	ar-rive
car-ry	nar-row	ar-row-root
mar-ry	spar-row	wheel-bar-row
tar-ry	bar-rel	bar-racks
Har-ry	gar-ret	bar-ri-er
Har-ri-et	Par-is	far-ri-er

Mam-ma took Har-ry to see a kind la-dy This la-dy led him in-to her gar-den. Har-ry heard screams in the trees. He look-ed up and saw a great many par-rots perch-ed up-on the branch-es. Some of the par-rots were green and some were grey; some were wild and some were tame. The la-dy said she li-ked to see the par-rots fly-ing a-bout.

Note.—*In these words* e *is sounded short,*
as in EN.

Cher-ry	ber-ry	per-ish
very	black-ber-ry	cher-ish
mer-ry	bil-ber-ry	her-ring
fer-ry	mul-ber-ry	Her-od
per-ry	cran-ber-ry	ter-ror
sher-ry	straw-ber-ry	ter-ri-fy
bu-ry	rasp-ber-ry	ter-ri-ble
cher-ub	bar-ber-ry	ter-ri-er

Har-ry ask-ed the la-dy whe-ther the par-rots ate up all the fruit.

"Yes," re-plied the la-dy, "they eat up all the fruit. There is not a cher-ry left in the gar-den, nor a plum, nor a peach, nor a straw-ber-ry, nor a rasp-ber-ry, nor a mul-ber-ry, nor a bar-ber-ry. The par-rots eat up every-thing—fruit and flow-ers."

Note.—*Tell the Child that* i *is not sounded like* i *in* fir *in these words, but like short* i.

	mir-a-cle	syr-up
Mir-ror	spir-it	syr-inge
Mir-i-am	squir-rel	myr-i-ad

Mir-i-am pick-ed a great many elder-ber-ries and some black sloes. She in-tend-ed to make a few bot-tles of wine. First, she squeez-ed out the juice of these ber-ries in-to a large ba-sin. She went to the cup-board for a spoon, and when she came back she found her bas-in quite emp-ty. A naugh-ty lit-tle boy had drunk up all this nice syr-up.

So poor Mir-i-am went with-out her nice wine.

Gree-dy Har-ry ought to have been a-sha-med of his con-duct.

NOTE.—*Let the Child be told that when o comes before a double r (or an r followed by a vowel), it is sounded short.*

Or-ange	mor-row	hor-rid
for-est	bor-row	hor-ror
cor-al	sor-row	hor-ri-ble
sor-rel	forē-head	Hor-ace

Hor-ace was of-ten al-low-ed to be in the gar-den by him-self. He was for-bid-den to eat any-thing with-out ask-ing leave.

One day his Mam-ma came in-to the gar-den. She saw that Hor-ace was eat-ing some-thing. When she ask-ed him what he was eat-ing, he re-pli-ed, "Nothing." So she de-sir-ed him to o-pen his mouth, and she found it full of a green stuff call-ed sor-rel.

"Well," said she, "I had an or-ange for you in my bas-ket, but since you like bit-ter sor-rel, I will not give you a nice or-ange."

NOTE.— *To teach the sound of u before double r,*
or r followed by a vowel.

	cur-ry	cour-age
Cur-rant	hur-ry	nour-ish
tur-ret	flur-ry	flour-ish
mur-rain	wor-ry	fur-ri-er

Once a good cler-gy-man a-woke in the night. How great was his ter-ror when he found the house was on fire. He had eight chil-dren. He fear-ed lest any of them should be burn-ed up. He went quick-ly to the nur-se-ry and burst o-pen the door. He found the nurse and five chil-dren sleep-ing in the room. He call-ed them to get up. and to hur-ry down-stairs. The nurse got up and car-ried the young-est in her arms, and she told the oth-er chil-dren to fol-low her as fast as they could.

But one of the chil-dren was still fast a-sleep, and he did not hear the nurse speak. So the poor lit-tle fel-low lay still in his bed, while all the rest got up and fol-low-ed the nurse down-stairs.

When they came to the street-door, they tri-ed to go out; but the wind beat the flames in their faces, and they found it hard to get out. Some of the chil-dren climb-ed out by the win-dows, and oth-ers went out through a lit-tle back door. At last the Pa-pa and Mam-ma and chil-dren were safe in the gar-den.

Pa-pa count-ed the chil-dren and found there were only seven, in-stead of eight.

John-ny was miss-ing.

Pa-pa look-ed up and saw John-ny stand-ing at the nur-se-ry win-dow, stretch-ing out his arms for help.

The lit-tle fel-low had a-wak-en-ed after the nurse left him. When he first woke he thought it was morn-ing, be-cause the room was light, and he call-ed for some one to take him up. But when he peep-ed through the cur-tains, and saw the flames on the ceil-ing, he was ter-ri-fied and ran to the door; but he could not get fur-ther, as the next room was in a blaze. Then he ran to the win-dow, but it was so high up that he could not see out, for John-ny was only six years old.

What could he do? He climb-ed up-on a chest, and look-ed out, and call-ed for some one to save him from the hor-ri-ble flames.

His fath-er saw him. He had the courage to try to run up-stairs; but the stairs were burn-ed up.

A man said, "I will fetch a lad-der."

An-o-ther man said, "There will be no time for that. I have thought of a way."

This man was tall and strong. He said. "I will stand a-gainst the wall, and a thin, tall man shall get on my shoul-ders, and he will be able to lift the child out of the win-dow."

They did so. John-ny had the cour-age to wait till the man got up and pull-ed him out. As soon as John-ny was safe in the man's arms, the roof fell in. John-ny would have been crush-ed, if he had been still in the house.

The man car-ried John-ny to a house where his pa-rents were. They had been full of hor-ri-ble fears, but when they saw John-ny they were full of joy. The fath-er said to his neigh-bours,—

"Let us kneel down and thank God, for though my house be burned, He has given me my eight chil-dren."

NOTE.— *In these words the first letters,* k, g, *and* w, *are not sounded.*

	knock	wrong	wrencl
Knife	knot	wrap	wretch
knave	knuc-kle	write	wrist
knead	gnat	wrote	wren
knee	gnash	wri-ter	wreck
kneel	gnaw	wreath	wrath

A wid-ow liv-ed in a small cot-tage wit her on-ly child. He was a boy of four yeaɪ old. Lit-tle Har-ry was a great com-fort t his poor moth-er.

The wid-ow work-ed hard to feed her-se and her boy. She knit-ted stock-ings, an sold them. In the e-ven-ing she taught poɑ boys to write. She went on mes-sa-ges fɑ her neigh-bours. Yet she could not get ɑ much mon-ey as she want-ed.

One e-ven-ing she was eat-ing her sup-per with Har-ry by her side. There was nothing for sup-per but a very lit-tle bread. As Har-ry was eat-ing his last mor-sel, he said to his moth-er, " What shall we do to-mor-row morn-ing? There is no bread in the house; we shall have no break-fast."

His moth-er re-plied, " Do not be a-fraid, Har-ry. God feeds the spar-rows: He will not for-get us. He has writ-ten in His Bi-ble, 'Ver-i-ly thou shalt be fed.' Kneel down, Har-ry, and pray God to have mer-cy up-on us, and to give us food."

So Har-ry knelt down and pray-ed for bread, and then went qui-et-ly to sleep in his bed.

Be-fore it was light in the morn-ing, Har-ry woke his moth-er, say-ing, " Moth-er, is the bread come?"

"No," said the moth-er, "the bread is not come yet; but it will come. Lie down, and go to sleep."

Poor lit-tle Har-ry was hun-gry, and that made him in such a hur-ry for the bread. Har-ry and his moth-er went to sleep a-gain.

Just as the sun was ri-sing, and all was light a-round, a knock was heard at the door A wo-man came in. She seemed in a hurry.

"Get up," she said to the wid-ow, "the farm-er's dairy-maid is very ill, and there is no one to milk the cows. Do come quick-ly, and milk them."

The poor wo-man dress-ed her-self quick-ly, and as she went out, she said to Har-ry, "Here, Har-ry, is bread for us: the farm-er will pay me well for milk-ing the cows."

The moth-er left lit-tle Har-ry in bed, prom-is-ing soon to come back with some break-fast. She went and milk-ed the cows The farm-er's wife ask-ed her to eat some break-fast. She sat down, but she could not eat, for she could not help think-ing of Har-ry.

The farm-er's wife said, " Why do you not eat ?"

The moth-er said that she had a lit-tle hun-gry boy at home, and that she wish-ed to take home her break-fast, if she might.

The farm-er's wife said, " Eat your own break-fast, and then you shall carry home some-thing for your boy."

The kind wo-man gave the moth-er plen-ty of bread and butter, and cheese, and meat, to take home. She wrap-ped them all in a cloth, and put them in-to a bas-ket. She gave the poor moth-er a can of milk be-sides.

Har-ry knelt down a-gain, and thank-ed God

	numb	high	neigh
Lamb	climb	nigh	weigh
crumb	comb	sigh	plough
dumb	limb	thigh	dough
thumb	tomb	Hugh	though

Eu-gene was a kind and gen-tle boy. He was fond of dumb an-i-mals. Birds and beasts are call-ed dumb an-i-mals, be-cause they can-not speak as we can.

Eu-gene had a pet lamb, and a tame can-a-ry. He was so kind to the old horse at plough, that the horse would neigh af-ter him when he pass-ed.

But he lov-ed his dog a-bove all That dog was a big, black, shag-gy dog, na-med Ben.

When Eu-gene was eight years old, he be-gan to go to a day-school. The school was three miles off. Eu-gene was not a-ble to walk so far. He would have li-ked to ride to school, but he had no po-ny. So what could he do?

The post-man, in a small cart, pass-ed by the house ev-e-ry day. So Eu-gene went with him in his cart. The post-man re-turn-ed in the af-ter-noon, and Eu-gene re-turn-ed too.

One day the post-man stop-ped at a house, and left Eu-gene in his cart at the gate. While Eu-gene was wait-ing there, he heard a sound like the howl-ing of a dog. He thought some dog was in pain. He ran down the field, and saw a troop of boys near a pond. They were duck-ing a poor dog in the water. They were pull-ing it out by a string, and then dip-ping it in—while the dog growl-ed and howl-ed.

Eu-gene was very sor-ry. He had the cōurage to say to these big boys, "Why do you treat the dog so ill?" Then he took out his knife and cut the string.

At the same time he clasp-ed the poor wet dog in his arms. The boys tried to snatch a-way the dog; but Eu-gene held it fast. Then a big boy push-ed Eu-gene in-to the wa-ter, and wet-ted him all o-ver. But the wa-ter was not deep, so Eu-gene got out.

All at once Ben was seen rush-ing to-wards the boys. That good dog had heard his mas-ter's voice, and was come to de-liv-er him from the wick-ed boys. He seiz-ed the big-gest boy by the leg with his teeth, and would not let him go. "Ben, Ben," cried Eu-gene, "you are come to help me."

And now a gen-tle-man ap-pear-ed. He was a friend of Eu-gene's. It was his dog that had been tor-ment-ed.

"Oh, Mop!" said the gen-tle-man, "poor Mop! what have these bad boys been do-ing to you?"

Very quick-ly the wick-ed troop ran off.

Eu-gene told the whole story to the gen-tle-man.

"You are a brave boy," said his friend. "Come home quick-ly, and change your wet clothes."

So he took him home, and told Eu-gene's pa-rents all that had hap-pen-ed. They were pleas-ed to hear of their boy's kind-ness to poor Mop. Soon af-ter-wards they gave Eu-gene a pret-ty po-ny, that he might ride to school, and ride home a-gain.*

* "Band of Hope Review."

Note.—In these words some of the letters are not sounded.

l *is not sounded.*	gh *is not sounded*	w *is not sounded.*
could	light	an-swer
would	night	sword
should	might	to-wards
walk	bright	
talk	de-light	r *is not sounded.*
stalk	straight	i-ron
chalk	eight	
calf	weight	h *is not sounded.*
half	caught	Thomas
balm	thought	Es-ther
calm	bought	
palm	fought	p *is not sounded.*
psalm	brought	cup-board
		rasp-ber-ry

l *and* f *are not sounded.*   d *is not sounded.*

half-pen-ny   Wed-nes-day

On Sun-day Es-ther sang psalms at church.
On Mon-day—she pick-ed rasp-ber-ries.
On Tues-day—she made rasp-ber-ry jam.
On Wed-nes-day—she bought eight large jars.
On Thurs-day—she fill-ed them with jam.
On Fri-day—she in-vi-ted eight-y chil-dren.
On Sa-tur-day—she gave them bread and jam
In Ja-nu-a-ry—boys make snow-balls.
In Fe-bru-a-ry—girls pluck snow-drops.
In March—high winds blow.
In A-pril—soft show-ers fall.
In May—hed-ges are cov-er-ed with blos-soms
In June—gar-dens are full of flow-ers.
In Ju-ly—reap-ers cut the corn.
In Au-gust—glean-ers pick up the ears.
In Sep-tem-ber—chil-dren pluck black-ber-ries.
In Oc-to-ber—cot-ta-gers ga-ther ap-ples.
In No-vem-ber—fogs dar-ken the air.
In De-cem-ber—the trees are with-out leaves.

Squir-rel

Clara had a squir-rel. It was a pret-ty lit-tle crea-ture, with a long tail and bright eyes. It was very fond of Clara, and knew her voice. When she call-ed " Coo chee, Coo-chee," it ran to her very fast. It bit her twice; but that was only in play. Once it bit her thumb, and once it bit her wrist. It lik-ed to climb up her dress, and sit upon her shoul-der.

It had a tall, round cage, with a long stick up the mid-dle. It used to run up and down this long stick. It slept in a bas-ket of hay at the bot-tom of the cage. There it lik-ed to lie curl-ed up un-der its long tail, and al-most hid-den among the hay. There was al-ways a ba-sin of bread and milk in the cage.

Clara used to give nuts to Coo-chee as a treat. Clara kept nuts in the pock-et of her dress. Coo-chee knew this; so he used to poke his head in-to her pock-et to find the nuts. It was droll to see his tail hang-ing out, while his whole bo-dy was hid-den in the pock-et. When Coo-chee had got the nut, he sat on Clara's shoul-der, crack-ed it with his teeth, and nib-bled it so slow-ly and so pret-ti-ly! When it had done eat-ing, it would run off and dart a-cross the floor, and climb up the cur-tains; and then it would run up and down the brass pole at the top of the cur-tain,—nor did its foot ever slip—nor did Coo-chee ever fall.

Coo-chee had a droll trick of hid-ing things. When it had eat-en nuts e-nough, it would hide the rest un-der the cloth on the ta-ble. Next day it did not for-get to look for its nuts, though it sel-dom found them.

Once Clara thought she would take Coo-chee out in the gar-den. She thought she could trust Coo-chee to come back when she call-ed him.

But Coo-chee soon ran up a very high tree, and would not come down. It was no use climb-ing up the tree, for Coo-chee quick-ly jump-ed off one tree on to an-o-ther. Clara brought a cup of bread and milk, and call-ed to Coo-chee. Coo-chee came down; but just as Clara was go-ing to catch him, he dart-ed off. At last night came, and Clara went home with-out Coo-chee.

Next morn-ing Clara went to seek for him; but she could not find him. An-oth-er day came, and an-oth-er day; but no Coo-chee. At last Clara said, "Coo-chee is lost. I shall nev-er see him a-gain."

Clara told ev-e-ry body she knew—that she had lost Coo-chee—for she ho-ped some-body might see him and bring him back.

A month pass-ed a-way, and no Coo-chee.

At last a gar-den-er came and ask-ed to speak to Clara. He said, "My la-dies were walk-ing in the gar-den, when a squir-rel came down from a high tree, and seem-ed quite tame, and we thought it might be your squir-rel that you lost.   And here it is in this bas-ket."

It was Coo-chee.   How glad Clara was, and how glad Coo-chee was!   The fool-ish lit-tle squir-rel was tir-ed of liv-ing in high trees, and go-ing with-out his din-ner ve-ry of-ten.   Yet Clara would not trust him out of doors any more.

At first Coo-chee was not so gay and play-ful as he used to be ; but soon he be-gan to play all his old tricks.

At last Clara went a long jour-ney, and she could not take Coo-chee.   She ask-ed the maids to take care of him.   The maids went in the fields to pick a-corns for him, and they gave him a great many—so many that he grew ill and died.   When Clara came back she found her Coo-chee stiff and cold.

long-er	young-er	an-ger
long-est	young-est	an-gry
strong-er	lin-ger	hun-ger
strong-est	night-in-gale	hun-gry
Fin-ger man-gle	sin-gle	Eng-land

Emily had two lit-tle green birds like par
rots, but much small-er. She did not keep
them in a cage, but she let them live on a
plant in the room. She li-ked to see them
climb from branch to branch with their hook-ed
beaks.

One day she took out her birds, perch-ed on
her fin-ger, in-to the gar-den. She knew that
they could not fly a-way, for their wings were
clip-ped. She put down her lit-tle par-rots on
the lawn, and stood close by to guard them ;
but she did not know that Puss lay hid in a
bush close be-hind. Puss was hun-gry, and
was ea-ger-ly watch-ing for a bird. When she

saw the pret-ty par-rots, she dart-ed out like a ti-ger, and pounc-ed up-on one of them. It was the young-est and the gen-tlest. In one mo-meat Puss was over the wall with her prey in her mouth.

Emily scream-ed with ter-ror. Her broth-er came out to see what was the mat-ter, but he could not help her. Puss was gone, and was be-gin-ning in some hid-ing-place to feast up-on the fa-vour-ite. Noth-ing was seen of that pret-ty bird but a few green feath-ers.

Emily was very an-gry with Puss. But it is of no use to be an-gry with beasts, for they have not sense to know right from wrong.

What be-came of Puss? Emily did not like to keep her any long-er, lest she should eat up the oth-er par-rot; so she sent the ser-vant with her to a for-est a great way off. The ser-vant took Puss there in a bas-ket and let her out.

NOTE.—*Tell the Child that* g *is soft before* e *and* i.

	hinge	cud-gel
	plunge	bad-ger
Pig-eon	sponge	Brid-get
sur-geon	loz-enge	Rog-er
dun-geon	por-ridge	George
le-gion	fid-get	Geor-gi-a-na
re-li-gion	bud-get	Geof-fry

A pig-eon loves its home. If you take it far from home, it will fly back a-gain very quick-ly. It knows the way home. It will fly over the sea, as well as the land.

Some-times a pig-eon is made to car-ry a let-ter like a post-man. The let-ter is fast-en-ed un-der the pig-eon's wing. Then the pig-eon is ta-ken to a place a-way from home. As soon as the pig-eon is let loose—it flies straight home with the let-ter.

Har-riet walk-ed out with her nurse and her lit-tle sis-ter Geor-gi-a-na. She came home, and knock-ed at the door. Geof-fry the foot-man o-pen-ed it, and said, "Some la-dies are here, and they have brought pres-ents for the chil-dren."

Har-riet was de-light-ed to hear this. As she went up-stairs she saw on a ta-ble in the pas-sage a very pret-ty toy. It was a lit-tle play-or-gan with three very small dan-cing dogs, not lar-ger than Har-riet's fin-ger, stand-ing on their hind legs, as if they were dan-cing, and a small man playing on a flute close by.

"Oh, I hope," thought Har-riet, "that toy is for me." But she said nothing.

She went in-to the draw-ing-room. The la-dies sent for the toys they had brought. They o-pen-ed a small par-cel, and took out a ba-by doll and a small cot, with some clothes for the doll to wear. They said to Har-riet, "We know you are fond of ba-bies, so we have brought this doll for you."

But Har-riet look-ed as if she did not like the pre-sent. "What is the mat-ter?" said the la-dies. "Do you not like this pret-ty doll?"

"No," said Har-riet in a low voice, "I want the oth-er toy."

The la-dies an-swer-ed, "We meant the oth-er toy for Geor-gi-a-na, be-cause she is young-er than you. Those dan-cing dogs are only fit for a very young child. You are five years old—Geor-gi-a-na is only three."

But Har-riet still said, "I should like to have the dan-cing dogs."

Then the la-dies gave her the lit-tle or-gan with the dan-cing dogs.

Har-riet went up-stairs much de-light-ed with her toy. But the nurse had been in the

room all the time. Nurse was an-gry with
Har-riet. She said, "How could you be so
naugh-ty? You ought to have ta-ken what
the la-dies brought for you!"

When Har-riet found that nurse was an-gry,
she be-gan to feel sor-ry that she had been so
wil-ful. She al-most wish-ed that she had
ta-ken the doll in-stead of the dogs. But now
it was too late to change. So Har-riet, with a
sad heart, turn-ed the han-dle of her or-gan
and made the dogs go round and round.

Why was Har-riet sad? Be-cause she had
been wil-ful. If the la-dies had said, "Which toy
will you have?" then she might have cho-sen
the dan-cing dogs. But they did not give her a
choice. So Har-riet ought to have ta-ken the
doll. She ought to have thank-ed the la-dies,
in-stead of say-ing, "I want the oth-er toy."

Geor-gi-a-na took the doll and was pleas-ed.

g before e sounds like j *in most words.*   *In these* g *sounds hard*

gem	gen-tle-man	get
gen-tle	gen-e-rous	for-get
Ger-ald	gen-e-ral	Ger-trude

g *sounds* j *in these words.*   g *sounds hard in these words*

gin	gi-raffe	gig	gir-dle
gin-gle	gi-ant	give	giz-zard
gib-bet	gin-ger	gift	gim-let
gib-let	gin-ger-bread	gild	gid-dy
gip-sy	gin-ger-cakes	gird	be-gin
Giles	gin-ger-wine	girl	Gil-bert

u *is sometimes put after* g *to make it sound hard*
In these words u *is not sounded.*

guard	guilt	rogue
guide	guilt-y	plague
guess	guin-ea	league
guest	gui-tar	di-a-logue

Ger-trude is a gen-tle girl.

Ger-ald is a gen-e-rous man.

Ger-trude plays on the gui-tar.

Ger-ald gave a guin-ea to a gip-sy.

Ger-trude show-ed me the gi-raffe.

Ger-ald bought gin-ger-bread for me.

Ger-trude was my guide in the wood.

Ger-ald was my guard in the crowd.

Ger-trude was my guest yes-ter-day.

Ger-ald will be my guest to-mor-row.

Gil-bert was the plague of his home.

He grew up to be a rogue.

He was guil-ty of many thefts.

He made a league with oth-er thieves.

At last he was guilt-y of mur-der.

He mur-der-ed a man with a gim-let.

He was hang-ed up-on a gib-bet.

Bridg-et was a gid-dy girl.

She drop-ped a gem in-to the riv-er.

Note.—Sc *are sounded before* e *and* i *like* s.

scene	scep-tre	as-cend
scent	scythe	des-cend

Scis-sors

sc *are sounded like* sk *before* a, o, *or* u.

scale	scour	Scotch-man
scab	scowl	scold-ing
scar	scourge	scuf-fle
scarf	scull	scut-tle
scare	scum	scare-crow
scald	Scotch	scat-ter
scoff	scorch	scar-let
scorn	scam-per	scaf-fold
scold	scant-y	scul-le-ry
scoop	scorn-er	scul-li-on
scales	scof-fer	scav-en-ger
scarce	scol-lop	coal-scut-tle

The scul-lion clean-ed the cop-per coal-scut-tle in the scul-lery.

The kit-chen-maid skim-med the scum off the broth.

The cook made the oys-ter scol-lops.

The dairy-maid scald-ed the milk-pans in the dairy.

The gar-den-er set up a scare-crow to scare a-way the birds from the cher-ries.

The house-maid scour-ed the stairs be-fore break-fast.

The laun-dress scorch-ed a mus-lin scarf with her hot i-ron by ac-ci-dent.

The nee-dle-wo-man cut out my dress with these scis-sors.

The groom scam-per-ed a-way on the grey horse. His horse rear-ed. He fell off and his head was cut o-pen, so that the scar may still be seen.

NOTE.—*Sometimes* ch *has the sound of* k.

School
k ch
sc sch

school-mas-ter	achc
school-fel-low	head-ache
schol-ar	an-chor
Christ-mas	chym-ist
Chris-ti-an	char-ac-ter
Chris-ti-a-na	mel-an-chol-y

Lit-tle Em-ma Vale liv-ed in a pret-ty vil-lage in the country. A ver-y old tree lifts up its tall head to the skies, and near it a ver-y old church lifts up its tall spire to the skies. Once there was no school-house in this vil-lage. Em-ma Vale, when she was very lit-tle, ran a-bout the vil-lage like a wild colt. Her clothes were in tat-ters, and her heart full of sin. But at last a good cler-gy-man came and built a school-house.

Lit-tle Em-ma was one of the schol-ars.

She learn-ed a-bout Christ. She be-came a Chris-ti-an child. Her heart and her char-ac-ter were chang-ed by the Ho-ly Spir-it.

One Mon-day morn-ing she was run-ning a-cross the green. A kind neigh-bour met her and gave her an ap-ple. Em-ma was much pleas-ed. She was a gen-e-rous child. She thought, "I will go and share my ap-ple with a school-fel-low in a cot-tage close by." She ran in-to the cot-tage. The lit-tle school-fel-low was there. He was a thought-less boy. A gun lay on the ta-ble. The boy did not know it was load-ed. He took it up and point-ed it at Em-ma. "I will shoot you," said he. He pull-ed the trig-ger. Em-ma fell down dead on the floor. O what a mel-an-chol-y e-vent! But not mel-an-chol-y to Em-ma; for her spir-it in a mo-ment as-cen-ded to her Sav-iour.

Su-gar

NOTE.—*In these words* s *has the sound of* sh.

| sure | sure-ly | su-gar-plum |
| as-sure | sure-ty | su-gar-can-dy |

Mar-y, Sar-ah, and Jes-sie, were three lit-tle sis-ters. They had no broth-er. They of-ten wish-ed they had a broth-er.

One day a let-ter came to their Pa-pa. It was from a friend of his. He said in the let-ter, "I am com-ing to see you, and I will bring my lit-tle boy with me." The three sis-ters were de-light-ed. They felt sure the boy would be like a broth-er to them.

At last the gen-tle-man ar-riv-ed and his son Lew-is with him. It was late in the even-ing. The girls were soon sent to bed, but be-fore they went up-stairs they saw Lew-is. When they were go-ing to bed, Mar-y said,

"Lew-is looks a bright, good-na-tured boy! Surely he will be kind to us!"

"O yes," said Sar-ah; "I am sure he will be just like a broth-er!"

The next morn-ing the three sis-ters saw Lew-is at break-fast. Af-ter-wards they were al-low-ed to play with him. They led him in-to the play-room and show-ed him their toys. Lew-is caught sight of a lit-tle play-dog He seiz-ed hold of it, say-ing, "May not I have this?" "You may have it in your hand," re-plied Mar-y, "but not to keep; for my cous-in Jen-ny gave it me, and now she's dead."

"But," cried Lew-is, "it is made of su-gar, and su-gar-dogs are made to be eat-en!" So say-ing, he bit off its head, and sat munch-ing it in his mouth. Mar-y said, "Are you like a broth-er? Before you came, we felt sure you would be, but you are not."

NOTE.—*In these words s has the hard sound of* zh

pleas-ure   treas-ure

dis-pleas-ure   leis-ure

Meas-ure

Ad-die was a lit-tle girl of six years old. It was her great pleas-ure to do what her pa-rents wish-ed.

Once she was in-vi-ted to dine out. Her Pa-pa took her to the house and left her there, quite a-lone, a-mongst strange gen-tle-men and la-dies. She knew one old gen-tle-man be-fore; he was a Gen-e-ral. His face was dark, with black hair. But Ad-die was not a-fraid, for he was kind. The old Gen-e-ral made Ad-die sit by his side at din-ner, and he cut up all her din-ner for her. He thought it a plea-sure to take care of her. There was a great many nice things on the ta-ble af-ter din-ner. There were su-gar-cakes and su-gar-can-dy; there were pre-serv-ed gin-ger and bran-dy-cherries; there were alm-onds and rai-sins, yet Ad-die would take noth-ing but a sponge-cake. She said that her Mam-ma would not al-low her to eat rich things, as they made her ill. The old Gen-e-ral gave her a sponge-cake. But when Ad-die was go-ing to eat it she saw there were cur-rants in it. So she laid it down, and said to the Gen-e-ral,—

"Mam-ma would not al-low me to eat this cake, as she does not think cur-rants good for me."

Then the Gen-e-ral took the cake and care-fully pull-ed out all the plums, and gave her the bits of cake one by one. He told her par-ents when he saw them that such an o-be-di-ent child was a treas-ure.*

* "The Floweret Gathered."—*Hatchard.*

NOTE.—Ph *has the sound of* f. *Let the Child call* ph— *as if it were* f.

	Jo-seph	pho-to-graph
Pheās-ant	or-phan	el-e-phant
Phe-be	proph-et	al-pha-bet
Phil-ip	se-raph	Phar-i-see
Phil-lis	phy-sic	So-phi-a
Ran-dolph	Pha-raoh	Sapph-i-ra
Al-phon-so	Hum-phrey	ep-i-taph

Phil-ip was a lit-tle boy of three years old. His mam-ma wish-ed to have his pho-to-graph ta-ken. But would Phil-ip stand still? Phil-ip prom-is-ed he would try to stand still.

Phil-ip walk-ed up some steps and came in-to the room. A kind, smi-ling gen-tle-man was there. He look-ed at Phil-ip and said, " I am a-fraid he is too young to stand still ; but I will try to take his like-ness."

Mam-ma took off Phil-ip's coat and hat, and show-ed him where to stand. Phil-ip tri-ed to stand still; but he mov-ed a lit-tle, and the pho-to-graph was spoil-ed.

"We will try once more," said the gen-tle-man.

"I am ti-red," said Phil-ip. So he sat in a chair, and threw him-self back.

The gen-tle-man said to Phil-ip, "Look at me." Phil-ip look-ed, and he saw a very pret-ty box. It had glass sides, and there were lit-tle dolls be-hind the glass. The gen-tle-man touch-ed the box, and the dolls moved up and down, and sweet mu-sic came out of the box. Phil-ip look-ed at the box with great de-light, and while he was look-ing his pho-to-graph was ta-ken. It was a nice pho-to-graph, just like Phil-ip: for this time he had not stir-red a foot or a hand.

The el-e-phant is the most sen-si-ble of all an-i-mals. He is more sen-sible than a dog. A tame el-e-phant will work for his mas-ter, as if he were a work-man. He can put bun-dles in-to boats with-out let-ting them get wet-ted.

El-e-phants do not eat men or beasts; but they eat corn, fruit, and ve-get-ables.

But what does the el-e-phant work with? Has he got hands? No; but he has some-thing like a hand, called a trunk, and with this he works; for he can twist his trunk round any-thing, and lift it up.

His trunk is called a pro-bos-cis.

An el-e-phant will car-ry men on his back There is no need to use a whip to make him go on, for he will obey his mas-ter's voice.

The el-e-phant is very kind and gen-tle.

There was an el-e-phant who lov-ed a lit-tle

child very much. The nurse used to bring the babe in its cra-dle, and place it near the el-e-phant. The el-e-phant took care of it while it slept, and drove off the flies from its face with his trunk; and when the child cried, he rock-ed the cra-dle. This el-e-phant grew so fond of this child, that at last he would nev-er eat his food, ex-cept the child were there.

An el-e-phant will nev-er hurt any one who does not hurt him; but he will re-venge an af-front. It is dan-ger-ous to mock him, or ill-treat him.

A man once took a co-coa-nut and struck it a-gainst an el-e-phant's forehead, mean-ing to break the shell. The next day the el-e-phant saw some co-coa-nuts on a stall in the street. He took up one with his trunk, and beat it a-bout the man's head.

The man died on the spot.

NOTE.—*Let the Child be taught that a has a peculiar sound at the end of words—a sound like neither the long or short sound of a.*

Go-ril-la.

um-brel-la	so-fa
al-pa-ca	chi-na.

Women's names ending in a.

A-da	E-va	E-li-sa
An-na	Em-ma	Re-bec-ca
Clar-a	El-la	Jo-an-na
Dor-a	Ro-sa	Ma-til-da
Flor-a	Mar-tha	Ag-ne-ta
Laur-a	Ber-tha	Au-gus-ta

Women's names ending in ia.

Ly-di-a	O-liv-i-a	Vic-tor-i-a
Ju-li-a	A-me-li-a	Eu-ge-ni-a
De-li-a	La-vin-i-a	Ce-cil-i-a

Women's names of four syllables ending in a.

Is-a-bel-la	Le-o-nor-a	Al-ex-an-dra

THE GO-RIL-LA.

Some black men heard a cry in a wood a lit-tle way off. They said to one an-o-ther, "Let us go and see who ut-ter-ed that cry." They went a-mong the trees, and walk-ed a-long till they saw a young go-ril-la sit-ting on the ground, eat-ing ber-ries. A lit-tle fur-ther on they saw a big go-ril-la. It was the moth-er of the lit-tle fel-low. They shot her with a gun, and down she fell from her branch quite dead. The lit-tle one saw his moth-er fall. It was a sad sight for him to see: for he had long clung to her back, as she climb-ed up the trees, and he had ta-ken many a ber-ry from her hand, and now he was left a moth-er-less mon-key.

He ran up a tree, and sat there and roar-ed. The black men could not reach him up so high: so they got an axe, and cut down the tree. Down came the tree with the ba-by go-ril-la. The black men rush-ed to-wards it, and threw a cloth o-ver its head and face to hin-der it from bi-ting them when they seiz-ed it. But it was such a fierce crea-ture that it bit through the cloth, and hurt the hand of one man and the leg of an-o-ther. Noth-ing could pre-vent its bit-ing, till the men got a strong fork-ed stick, and fas-ten-ed the crea-ture's head in the fork-ed part. In this way they lift-ed it up to car-ry it to their ca-noe, or boat. The ba-by go-ril-la was a-bout as tall as a child of two years old, and it was not heav-y to lift up.

There was a gen-tle-man in the ca-noe, He was a white man trav-el-ling a-bout. He was very glad to see the lit-tle go-ril-la, for he want-ed to have one to keep as a pet.

THE YOUNG GO-RIL-LA.

The go-ril-la bel-low-ed as he was lift-ed in-to the boat, and look-ed wild-ly a-bout with his wick-ed lit-tle eyes. The men quick-ly got some thin sticks, call-ed bam-boos, and made them in-to a cage. When the lit-tle crea-ture was safe-ly shut up in his cage, ev-e-ry one came to look at him.

What sort of a crea-ture was he? A strong, ac-tive fel-low, with a black face and black hands. The rest of his body was cov-er-ed with grey hair and dark hair.

The gen-tle-man came close to the cage, and spoke kind-ly to the lit-tle pri-son-er; but the go-ril-la rush-ed at the bars of the cage, and bel-low-ed. Then he thrust out one foot, and caught hold of the gen-tle-man's trou-sers, and tore them, and then crouch-ed up in a cor-ner of the cage, and sat there look-ing wick-ed-ly with his small grey eyes.

The gen-tle-man sent the men to pick some ber-ries. He put the ber-ries with a cup of wa-ter in-to the cage, but the go-ril-la would not touch any food while any one was near.

The gen-tle-man gave him the name of Joe. Next day he found Joe had eat-en and drunk a lit-tle, and was grown fier-cer than ev-er— rush-ing at ev-e-ry one who came near the cage.

He threw some of Joe's fa-vour-ite leaves in-to his cage. Joe ate them, but did not seem in a bet-ter tem-per than be-fore. On the third day he was still an-gry—bel-low-ing, rush-ing, or sulk-ing in a cor-ner.

The fourth day, when the gen-tle-man came to see his pet, he found the cage EMP-TY!! He felt sure that Joe had got a-way by squeez-ing his body be-tween the bam-boos.

All the men cried out, "Let us go in-to the woods and bring him back." But the mas- ter said, "Stop a mo-ment: I may want my gun. I will fetch it." So he went in-to his bed-room to get it.

Sud-den-ly he heard a growl come from un- der his bed. He knew Joe's voice. He call-ed to the blacks; they rush-ed in, and Joe crept out from his hi-ding-place,—his eyes gla-ring with rage. The men shut the win-dows that Joe might not es-cape; but they were a-fraid lest Joe should fall up-on them and bite them, and so they went out and left him a-lone.

The gen-tle-man was a-fraid that Joe would hurt his fur-ni-ture, and per-haps des-troy his tick-ing clock. He and his men soon came back with a large net. They all threw it o-ver Joe. Four men held him fast,—in spite of his roar-ing and kick-ing. The cage had been

mend-ed, and the bam-boos placed more close-ly
to-geth-er. Joe was push-ed in, and the net
ta-ken a-way. Great was Joe's rage at find-ing
him-self a-gain in his cage.

His mas-ter kept Joe with-out food for a
day and a night. He thought Joe might grow
tame, if half-starved. Joe was a lit-tle bet-ter
in the morn-ing; for he took some ber-ries
out of his mas-ter's hand. But he was not
re-al-ly tame. He went on tear-ing his mas-ter's
clothes with his foot, when-ev-er he could.
He be-hav-ed still worse to the blacks.

He had a half-bar-rel for his bed. It was
fill-ed with hay. It was a-mu-sing to see Joe
at night shake up the hay to make his bed com-
fort-a-ble, and then creep in-to the bar-rel, and
cov-er him-self up with hay.

He would eat nothing but leaves and
berries.

The gen-tle-man be-gan to fear he should nev-er suc-ceed in ta-ming Joe

One day when he went to feed him, he found his cage EMP-TY a-gain! This time Joe had gnaw-ed the bam-boos, and made a hole through which he had es-caped. He had on-ly just got out: his mas-ter saw him run-ning on all-fours to-wards the woods.

The gentleman call-ed to the black men. More than a hundred came and pur-sued Joe. The crea-ture yell-ed with rage, and ran at one fel-low and threw him down. Other men spread the net o-ver naugh-ty Joe. Four men brought him back—bi-ting and kick-ing.

This time chains were put on him. With chains he was fas-tened to the cage—so that he nev-er could es-cape any more.

But he soon fell sick and DIED.

This was the end of the fierce little go-ril-la.

THE PET-LAMB.

Some child-ren had a pet-lamb call-ed Dai-sy. Their moth-er could get no work to do. She sold her things to get money. At last she had no-thing left to sell but the pet-lamb. She went to the butch-er and ask-ed him to buy the lamb. The butch-er said, " Here is a pound, and I will fetch the lamb to-mor-row." To-mor-row he came. The child-ren were play-ing with Dai-sy. "I am come for the lamb," said the man. The child-ren cri-ed out, " O moth-er, you will not sell our lamb?" The moth-er said, " I have no food, I must sell it." The child-ren knelt round their moth-er cry-ing, "Don't sell it." The mother, with tears, gave back the pound to the butch-er, say-ing, " I will keep the lamb a lit-tle lon-ger." The kind butch-er said, " Keep both the lamb and the pound."

NOTE.—*Let the Child be taught that* tion *is
sounded as if spelt* shon.

Words of THREE SYLLABLES.

At-ten-tion	do-na-tion	tempt-a-tion
af-fec-tion	ex-er-tion	in-ten-tion
af-flic-tion	e-rup-tion	pro-tec-tion
re-la-tion	in-fec-tion	sal-va-tion
de-tec-tion	pro-duc-tion	vex-a-tion
di-rec-tion	re-demp-tion	car-na-tion

Words of FOUR SYLLABLES *ending in* TION.

in-cli-na-tion	con-ver-sa-tion
in-ter-rup-tion	sep-a-ra-tion
oc-cu-pa-tion	con-fla-gra-tion
pro-vo-ca-tion	con-dem-na-tion
re-sur-rec-tion	con-so-la-tion
sit-u-a-tion	con-gre-ga-tion
suf-fo-ca-tion	con-tra-dic-tion
in-un-da-tion	hab-it-a-tion
des-o-la-tion	ed-u-ca-tion

Phe-be went to pay a vis-it to a re-la-tion in the coun-try. Be-fore she went her moth-er gave her this di-rec-tion: " Do not pick fruit in the gar-den, but be sat-is-fied with what is given you."

Phe-be as-sur-ed her moth-er it was her in-ten-tion to o-bey. One af-ter-noon Phe-be had no oc-cu-pa-tion in her re-la-tion's house, and she wan-der-ed all a-lone a-bout the gar-den. She came to a green door; she o-pen-ed it, and found her-self in a gar-den full of fruits. Her eyes were soon fix-ed up-on some red cher-ries grow-ing on the wall.

Phe-be ought to have left such a scene of tempt-a-tion. But she fol-low-ed her in-cli-na-tion, and took two cher-ries. She left the gar-den with the sad re-flec-tion that she had been dis-o-be-dient. She felt a-fraid of de-tec-tion, and full of vex-a-tion.

NOTE.—Sion *at the end of a word is usually sounded* shon.

| man-sion | oc-ca-sion | as-cen-sion |
| pen-sion | ex-cur-sion | a-ver-sion |

In many words the syllable before sion, tion, *and* xion, *is joined with these syllables.*

passion	mission	trans-gression
com-passion	per-mission	pos-session
con-fession	pe-tition	cru-ci-fixion

ous *at the end of a word is sounded* us.

jeal-ous	nu-me-rous	cour-a-geous
en-vi-ous	glo-ri-ous	dan-ger-ous
glut-ton-ous	mis-chiev-ous	bois-ter-ous

tious, cious, *and* xious, *are sounded* shus.

| gra-cious | frac-tious | au-da-cious |
| an-xious | cau-tious | fe-ro-cious |

The syllable before tious *or* cious *is often joined to it.*

| precious | ma-licious | de-licious |

THE RE-SUR-REC-TION.

The Lord Je-sus was cru-ci-fied by wick-ed men; but he was not bu-ried by wick-ed men. A good man, nam-ed Jo-seph, wish-ed to get pos-session of his Lord's body. So he went to Pon-tius Pi-late with this pe-tition, "Let me have the body of Je-sus."

Pon-tius Pi-late gave him per-mission to take down the dead body from the cross.

Jo-seph wrap-ped that precious body in fine lin-en with sweet spi-ces. He brought it in-to his own gar-den, and laid it in his own new tomb. That tomb was hewn out of the side of a rock. No dead body had ever been laid in that dark man-sion.

Some wo-men, who felt much af-fec-tion for their Lord, went home to pre-pare sweet oint-ment for his dead body.

But there were some wick-ed men who went to Pon-tius Pi-late, and ask-ed him to set sol-diers to watch near the tomb, lest the dis-ci-ples should steal the body of Jesus.

So Pi-late gave them per-mission to set sol-diers to watch near the tomb.

These en-vi-ous, ma-licious men soon got some sol-diers to keep watch.

But the sol-diers watch-ed only one night. Ear-ly in the morn-ing, be-fore it was light, an an-gel des-cend-ed from Heav-en, and roll-ed a-way the stone from the door of the tomb. And there was a great earth-quake. The sol-diers trem-bled and shook from fear. They fell back, and lay still like dead men; but at last they got up, and ran trem-bling to the cit-y.

And now some women came with jars of sweet oint-ment. They were sur-pri-sed to see the great stone roll-ed a-way. They went in-to the tomb, and saw an an-gel sit-ting there, clo-thed in white. At first they were fright-en-ed; but the an-gel said,—

"Fear not: you are look-ing for Je-sus, who was cru-ci-fied. He is not here, for He is ris-en. Go quick-ly and tell His dis-ci-ples that He is ris-en from the dead."

As the wo-men were run-ning to tell the dis-ci-ples of the re-sur-rec-tion, Je-sus met them. They held him by the feet, and wor-ship-ped him.

Jesus said to them, "Be not a-fraid; go tell my broth-ers to go to Gal-i-lee;—there they shall see me."

The women went and told the dis-ci-ples what Je-sus had said.

So the dis-ci-ples went to a moun-tain in Gal-i-lee, and saw their be-lov-ed Mas-ter. ris-en from the dead, nev-er to die a-gain.

NOTE.—*Let the Child now be taught the power of accent, and let him be shown how to lay a great stress on the accented Syllables.*

Words accented on the FIRST SYLLABLE.

ab-sent	fil-bert	dar-ling	har-vest
beau-ty	sum-mer	drum-mer	hatch-et
bis-cūit	win-ter	emp-ty	mor-sel
cus-tard	stud-y	naugh-ty	whole-some
ap-ple	bod-y	pil-low	tire-some
chap-ter	mur-der	shel-ter	loi-ter
Bi-ble	pris-on	clev-er	mu-sic

The following words are accented on the LAST SYLLABLE.

ab-surd	be-cause	mis-take	un-kind
a-bode	be-come	pre-pare	un-true
a-live	com-mit	re-main	un-ripe
ad-vice	con-ceal	re-joice	un-safe
en-joy	de-part	re-fuse	ap-pear
em-ploy	de-ceive	re-quest	pro-voke
an-noy	de-light	un-bar	pro-vide
ba-boon	dis-turb	un-dress	im-mense

GEORGE'S WHEEL-BAR-ROW.

(MI-NUTE *is sounded as if spelt* min-nit.)

George was the son of a poor wid-ow. He
had no fath-er, and he was the eld-est boy.
It was his du-ty to help his moth-er as much
as he was a-ble. His un-cle liv-ed in a cot-tage
at a lit-tle dis-tance, and this un-cle was very
gen-e-rous to the wid-ow and her chil-dren.

When George was sev-en, his un-cle brought
him a birth-day pres-ent. It was a lit-tle
wheel-bar-row, paint-ed red and green. George
was de-light-ed, and he prom-is-ed his moth-er
to wheel ev-e-ry-thing for her that she want-ed.
He oft-en ask-ed her, " Have you noth-ing for
me to wheel?" And when his moth-er said
"No," he was very sor-ry.

One day his moth-er took him with her to
mar-ket, and let him wheel a heap of ap-ples
to sell there.

 She told him he
had wheel-ed the ap-
ples so well that she
should soon take him
with her to the mill,
as she want-ed to
buy some flour.

The next day aft-er go-ing to mar-ket
George met a boy he knew call-ed Jo-seph.
This boy had a big, black dog. When he saw
the wheel-bar-row, he pro-po-sed to tie the dog
to the bar-row. George said he was a-fraid
lest the dog should bite. Jo-seph laugh-ed at
him for be-ing a-fraid of a dog.

So the boys got some rope, and tried to
fas-ten the dog to the bar-row. At this mo-
ment George heard his moth-er call-ing him.

"Don't go," said Jo-seph.

"I must go in a min-ute," said George.

Soon his lit-tle sis-ter Ma-ry came run-ning, say-ing, "Moth-er wants you this min-ute. Un-cle will dine with us to-mor-row, be-cause it is his birth-day, and moth-er wants to go to the mill to fetch flour to make cakes for him and lit-tle cou-sins. So go this min-ute with your bar-row, like a dear, good boy."

"In a min-ute," said George.

Min-ute aft-er min-ute slip-ped by, and moth-er was ti-red of wait-ing: so she took a large bas-ket on her arm, and set out by her-self. But she soon turn-ed back, for she heard a loud scream—the dog had bit-ten George, and thrown him in the mud!

Moth-er ran to help him up, and took him in-to the house, and put a poul-tice on the bite. George cried and said, "I will nev-er dis-o-bey you a-gain, dear moth-er. I will always come the min-ute you call me. Do for-give me!"

Words accented on the FIRST SYLLABLE.

Tes-ta-ment	mis-e-ry	care-ful-ly
pun-ish-ment	mem-o-ry	faith-ful-ly
poss-i-ble	van-i-ty	min-is-ter
sen-si-ble	en-e-my	pris-on-er
beau-ti-ful	cu-ri-ous	fool-ish-ness
du-ti-ful	fu-ri-ous	i-dle-ness
ap-pe-tite	mul-ti-tude	spec-ta-cles
croc-o-dile	grat-i-tude	dif-fi-cult

Words accented on the SECOND SYLLABLE.

un-ru-ly	de-par-ture	e-lev-en
un-ho-ly	de-liv-er	e-nor-mous
un-god-ly	de-ter-mine	en-tan-gle
o-bli-ging	dis-hon-est	em-ploy-ment
al-low-ance	e-ter-nal	a-bun-dance

Words accented on the THIRD SYLLABLE.

af-ter-noon	re-com-mend	dis-ap-point
en-ter-tain	re-col-lect	dis-ap-prove
in-ter-fere	un-der-stand	con-tra-dict

Cha-rac-ters of Beasts.

The dog is faith-ful.
The cat is clean.
The fox is cun-ning
The hare is tim-id.
The cow is qui-et.
The ass is pa-tient.
The horse is ea-ger.
The sheep is harm-less.
The goat is nim-ble.
The pig is glut-ton-ous.
The squir-rel is play-ful.
The mon-key is mis-chiev-ous
The camel is ob-sti-nate,
The bear is sul-ky.
The lion is fe-ro-cious.
The ti-ger is ma-licious.
The wolf is vo-ra-cious.
The el-e-phant is sa-ga-cious.

Cha-rac-ters of Birds.

The dove is gen-tle.

The par-rot is talk-a-tivē.

The goose is sil-ly.

The can-a-ry is spright-ly.

The cuck-oo is treāch-er-ous.

The lark is mer-ry.

The owl is grave.

The spar-row is pert.

The rob-in is so-ci-a-ble.

The chick-en is self-ish.

The mag-pie is dis-hon-est

The ea-gle is da-ring.

Cha-rac-ters of In-sects.

The bee is dil-i-gent.

The wasp is spite-ful.

The ant is care-ful.

The spi-der is skil-ful.

though
sounded tho.

thought
sounded thaut.

through
sounded thru.

The lion is not so big as the el-e-phant; but he is more ter-ri-ble, for he de-vours an-i-mals, while the e-le-phant lives up-on ve-ge-ta-bles. Yet, though he is very fe-ro-cious, he is some-times very af-fec-tion-ate.

There once was a lion kept in a den. His keep-er was ta-ken ill, and could not at-tend up-on him as u-sual. An-oth-er per-son came to feed the lion in-stead. But the lion would not eat; he only bel-low-ed at the stran-ger. It seem-ed as if he thought his keep-er was dead. But the keep-er soon got well, and came and look-ed at the lion through the bars of the den. The lion start-ed up full of joy, and lick-ed the keep-er's face through the bars. Then the keep-er went in-to the den, and ca-ress-ed the af-fec-tion-ate beast.

Words of FOUR SYLLABLES *accented on the First.*

a-mi-a-ble	com-fort-a-ble	dil-i-gent-ly
val-u-a-ble	ve-ge-ta-ble	gen-e-ral-ly
mis-e-ra-ble	cat-er-pil-lar	reg-u-lar-ly

Accented on the Second Syllable.

a-gree-a-ble	a-rith-me-tic	im-per-ti-nent
ex-cu-sa-ble	as-tron-o-my	in-dus-tri-ous
un-du-ti-ful	par-tic-u-lar	o-be-di-ent
un-mer-ci-ful	im-pos-si-ble	com-pan-i-on

Accented on the Third Syllable.

al-to-geth-er   ev-er-last-ing   dis-ap-point-ment

Accented on the Fourth Syllable.

nev-er-the-less   su-per-in-tend   mis-rep-re-sent

Words of FIVE SYLLABLES *accented on the Second.*

im-me-di-ate-ly	per-am-bu-la-tor
par-tic-u-lar-ly	af-fec-tion-ate-ly

Accented on the Third.

dis-o-be-di-ent	op-por-tu-ni-ty
zo-o-lo-gi-cal	pos-si-bil-i-ty

An Ar-tist draws and paints pic-tures.
A Bra-zi-er makes things of brass.
A Car-pen-ter makes things of wood.
A Dec-o-ra-tor a-dorns hou-ses.
An En-gra-ver makes prints from pic-tures.
A Far-ri-er shoes hor-ses.
A Gro-cer sells tea, cof-fee, and su-gar.
A Hab-er-dash-er sells rib-bons and lace.
An I-ron-mon-ger sells things of i-ron.
A Jew-el-ler deals in pre-ci-ous stones.
A La-bour-er works for his mas-ter.
A Ma-son makes things of stone.
A Nail-er makes i-ron in-to nails.
An O-ver-seer su-per-in-tends la-bour-ers.
A Po-lice-man guards us from thieves.
A Sta-tion-er sells pa-per and pens.
A Tai-lor cuts out cloth in-to clothes.
An Up-hol-ster-er hangs up cur-tains.
A Wheel-wright makes wheels for car-ria-ges.

Ar-chi-bald is af-fec-tion-ate.

Be-a-trix is ben-e-vo-lent.

Chris-to-pher is cha-ri-ta-ble.

Do-ro-the-a is du-ti-ful.

E-lis-a-beth is ex-cel-lent.

Fred-e-ric is for-giv-ing.

Ge-rald-ine is gen-e-rous.

Hen-ri-et-ta is hum-ble.

Is-a-bel is in-dus-tri-ous.

Kath-a-rine is kind-heart-ed.

Le-o-pold is lib-e-ral.

Mil-li-cent is mer-ci-ful.

Ol-iv-er is o-be-di-ent.

Pris-cil-la is pa-ti-ent.

Re-gi-nald is re-spect-ful.

Se-bas-tian is sin-cere.

The-re-sa is ten-der-heart-ed.

U-ra-ni-a is use-ful.

Val-en-tine is vir-tu-ous.

THE LOST CHIL-DREN.

Aus-tra-li-a is a very large coun-try. It is not full of peo-ple like Eng-land. A per-son may walk many miles with-out see-ing a man or wo-man, a house or gar-den. There are few roads in parts of Aus-tra-li-a. Peo-ple of-ten wan-der a-bout with-out a path, and they of-ten lose their way, and can-not get home a-gain.

A poor man, named Mr. Duff, liv-ed in a cot-tage, with his wife and three chil-dren.

He was a car-pen-ter, and he of-ten built cot-ta-ges for Eng-lish peo-ple just come o-ver **to** the new land. His three lit-tle chil-dren were call-ed I-sa-ac, Jane, and Frank.

I-sa-ac and Frank were boys, and Jane was a girl. I-sa-ac was nine, Jane was sev-en, and Frank was only three.

One day their moth-er, Mrs. Duff, de-sir-ed the lit-tle boys to go out and pick broom. The two boys had been used to pick broom, and they had al-ways come home safe-ly.

This time I-sa-ac beg-ged his moth-er to al-low Jane to come with him as well as Frank.

"O! moth-er," cried he, "do let her come. I want to show her pret-ty flow-ers that I have found in the wood. Do let her come with us, and we will bring you bet-ter broom than we ever brought home be-fore."

" Well," said the moth-er, " you may go, as you wish it so par-tic-u-lar-ly."

After break-fast the hap-py lit-tle ones set out with a string to tie up the broom. They were full of mirth, and lit-tle thought of the pos-si-bil-i-ty of being lost on the heath.

They went im-me-di-ate-ly to a lit-tle hill on the heath; then they scram-bled over a fence into a field where beau-ti-ful wild flow-ers grew a-mong the broom. Here they play-ed a-bout till they thought it was time to re-turn. But they had for-got-ten on which side they had en-ter-ed, and they went over the fence on the wrong side.

And now they wan-der-ed far-ther and far-ther from home, till they grew hun-gry and tired.

They cried out as loud as pos-si-ble,

" Coo-ey, Coo-ey!" but no one was near e-nough to hear them.

Mean-while their pa-rents grew un-ea-sy.

" Why have not the chil-dren re-turn-ed?" said the fath-er to the moth-er.

" I fear they have lost their way," re-plied the moth-er.

" Let us go and look for them," said they.

They went and search-ed ev-e-ry-where. They ask-ed their neigh-bours to help them. " Coo-ey, coo-ey," sound-ed all o-ver the heath, but no an-swer came. The pa-rents grew mis-e-ra-ble from anx-i-e-ty. They search-ed till the sun-set, and then they search-ed till the moon went down, and left them in mid-night dark-ness. Then they went home, but not to sleep, for they could not shut their eyes.

Next morn-ing it was Sat-ur-day, and they search-ed a-gain. They look-ed on the ground for marks of lit-tle feet—they could see no foot-steps. Men on horse-back came from dis-tant places. They gal-lop-ed over the coun-try calling, " Coo-ey, coo-ey."

On Sat-ur-day there was a dread-ful storm. Tor-rents of rain pour-ed down. The mis-e-ra-ble pa-rents shud-der-ed to think of the mis-e-ry of their lit-tle ones.

Sun-day pass-ed a-way and Mon-day came.

Now the neigh-bours be-gan to think the chil-dren must have per-ish-ed in the wet and the cold.

But on Mon-day ev-en-ing two men found some lit-tle foot-steps on the heath. These lit-tle steps were ten miles from the chil-dren's home. They were pre-cious marks ! The men who found them slept on the ground near the marks, lest they should for-get where they were.

On Tues-day one of the men went to tell his com-pan-ions of the new-found steps. Many peo-ple has-ten-ed to the place, and search-ed dil-i-gent-ly for more steps. But soon the dark-ness of night stop-ped the search.

An-oth-er storm of rain a-rose that night.

Next day men search-ed a-gain. Great was the dis-ap-point-ment of the men to find no more foot-steps. The rain had wash-ed them all a-way.

Wed-nes-day and Thurs-day were spent in look-ing for the lost chil-dren. Many now said, "They must be dead." Nev-er-the-less the fa-ther hop-ed they were still alive. He thought he would ask some black men to help him to find them ; for he knew that black men were clev-er in find-ing foot-steps. He went a long way on horse-back to fetch the black men.

On Fri-day night the fa-ther came back to the heath with three black men, call-ed Dick-ey, Jer-ry, and Fred. These blacks soon found many marks of the chil-dren's wan-der-ings; they found marks of their feet and of their bodies where they had sat or lain down.

"Here," said Dick-ey, "lit-tle one was tired. Here he sat down. Big one kneel down, — car-ry him a-long."

Then Jer-ry said, "Here chil-dren trav-el all night—dark—not see bush; SHE fall down on bush."

"Here," said Fred, "lit-tle one tired a-gain; big one kneel down,—no a-ble to rise,—fall flat on his face."

It was the marks on the ground which show-ed the blacks what the chil-dren had done; but white men could not see all those marks.

At last the blacks came to a place just like

the heath near the chil-dren's home. The lit-tle ones had thought they were near home, and they had gath-er-ed broom and tied it up, but soon they had been dis-ap-point-ed, for no home was near, and they had thrown a-way their broom! Poor chil-dren!

And now Sat-ur-day came again. Eight days the chil-dren had been lost, but the fa-ther con-tin-u-ed to place his trust in God. A white man found some fresh steps on Sat-ur-day af-ter-noon. These steps led to a lit-tle nook or thick-et where the chil-dren had slept the night be-fore, but now the place was emp-ty. No foot-steps could be seen, only the marks of the chil-dren's bod-ies on the ground.

The fa-ther knew not which way to go, so he let his horse go which way it pleas-ed, and he trust-ed in God to lead it a-right. The horse set off in a can-ter, and brought the fa-ther to a place where fresh foot-steps were seen.

The fa-ther rode on till he came to a lit-tle hill, and from the top look-ed all around. He saw a lit-tle clump of trees, like those un-der which the chil-dren had slept. He rode im-me-di-ate-ly to-wards the leaf-y nook. As he rode he saw some-thing like clothes flut-ter-ing in the wind. He gal-lop-ed, full of hope, to-wards the spot, and he was not dis-ap-point-ed.

Be-neath the boughs, on a heap of broom, the CHIL-DREN WERE SLEEP-ING!!

The young-est lay be-tween the other two, as if to be kept warm. The fa-ther could not wake them, but many ri-ders came gal-lop-ing up, and other men came run-ning, and a-woke the chil-dren by their noise.

I-sa-ac tried to sit up. Oh, how thin and pale was his face! How wild his eyes look-ed!

But they were fix-ed on his fa-ther. He tried to speak, but his tongue was so dry that he could only faint-ly ut-ter "Father," and then he fell back.

Lit-tle Frank was much bet-ter, for his broth-er had of-ten car-ried him, and his sis-ter had wrap-ped him in her own frock. Frank cried out, "Fa-ther, why did not you come for us soon-er,—we were coo-ey-ing for you?"

Jane was the worst of all, for she too had of-ten car-ried Frank, and had strip-ped her-self of her frock to cov-er him. Her eyes were shut, and her lips could only ut-ter, "Cold, cold!" while she lay with her hands curl-ed up and shiv-er-ing.

The men had brought no food for the chil-dren, for they had thought only dead bod-ies would be found. But one of the men had a piece of bread and but-ter, and a bit of gin-ger

root in his pock-et. The chil-dren were fed
with ti-ny mor-sels, as they lay in the arms of
the kind men, who car-ried them a-long.

It was eight miles to the near-est hut.

It was dark be-fore the chil-dren were
brought to the door.

A kind wo-man came out and beg-ged the
men to bring in the lit-tle ones. She laid them
all side by side in a soft and warm bed.

Soon lit-tle Jane's voice was heard in bed
re-peat-ing her ev-en-ing pray-er,—

> "Gentle Jesus, meek and mild,
> Look upon a little child."

That lit-tle girl had nev-er for-got-ten to
say her pray-ers ev-e-ry night and morn-ing
while lost up-on the heath. Her broth-ers
had heard her, and God had heard her, and
had sent a de-liv-er-er when the lit-tle wan-
der-ers were read-y to die.

U

THE AS-CEN-SION.

Af-ter Christ rose from the dead, He was seen by his friends for for-ty days. At the end of for-ty days He went back to hea-ven.

His go-ing back to hea-ven is call-ed His As-cen-sion.

Who saw Him as-cend to hea-ven? His dis-ci-ples. He had been walk-ing with them, He had been talk-ing to them. He was lifting up his hands and bless-ing them —when— all at once—He was ta-ken up, and a cloud bore Him a-way out of sight.

It was on a moun-tain that the dis-ci-ples were stand-ing when Je-sus went up to hea-ven: that moun-tain's name was Ol-i-vet.

The dis-ci-ples saw Je-sus go-ing up, and they kept look-ing and look-ing, till they could see Him no more.

They were still look-ing up to the sky, when they heard a gen-tle voice speak-ing to them.

Whose voice was it?

The dis-ci-ples look-ed and saw two men stand-ing by them. These men were dressed in gar-ments white as snow. But they on-ly seem-ed to be men—they were AN-GELS.

The an-gels said to the dis-ci-ples,—

" Why do you stand look-ing up in-to

hea-ven ? This same Je-sus who is ta-ken up from you in-to hea-ven will come back in the same way as you have seen him go into hea-ven."

Will Je-sus in-deed re-turn to this world ?

O yes, He will some day re-turn. We do not know which day. He will come back in clouds, and an-gels with Him, and He will stand up-on Mount Ol-i-vet. Yes, those feet that were nail-ed to the cross will stand upon that Mount.

NOTE.— *The Child will improve from reading daily a portion of the* LISTS OF WORDS *in this volume—while he practises reading in other books of amusing narratives.*

When perfected in reading, it will be soon enough to learn to spell without a book. The lists in this volume may then be his spelling lessons. Afterwards—" BUTTER'S SPELLING-BOOK," *or* 'THE SPELLING-BOOK SUPERSEDED,' *will perfect the pupil in spelling.*

London Printed by STRANGEWAYS & SONS. Tower Street, Cambridge Circus W.C.

Works by the same Author.

A New Illustrated Nursery Gift-Book for the very Little Ones.

THE PEEP OF DAY;

OR,

A SERIES OF THE EARLIEST RELIGIOUS INSTRUCTION THE
INFANT MIND IS CAPABLE OF RECEIVING.

In a large type, and with Thirteen Coloured Illustrations. Impl. 16mo. 5s.
New Edition, Illustrated, Imperial 16mo. 2s. 6d.
Also, 18mo. 27 Illustrations, cloth, 2s.; roxburghe, 2s. 6d.
Cheap School Edition, with 27 Illustrations, limp, 1s. 2d.
Popular Edition, for use of Schools, limp, 6d.

ABOUT a million copies of this Book (published originally in
1833) have been sold in England at 2s. and 1s. 2d. There have
been editions printed and sold by thousands in America; and the
Work has been translated and published in French, German, Russian,
Samoan, Chinese, and many other languages, both for Missionary and
general Educational use.

The Indian Government, in their Educational Report for April,
1873, specially recommended the Work for use in their Mission-
schools; and Missionaries have testified to the fact that, by having
the Book in English, and translating it verbatim, they have been
enabled to bring the truths of the Bible within the comprehension,
and home to the hearts of the heathen, when their own explanations
have failed.

A Handsome Presentation Box for the Young.

With 340 Illustrations and 7 Maps.

THE PEEP OF DAY SERIES.

BEST EDITION, Ten 18mo. volumes, roxburghe, gilt edges, in box, 31s. 6d.

CONTENTS.

The Peep of Day.

Streaks of Light.

Line upon Line. 2 Vols.

Precept upon Precept.

Apostles Preaching.

Lines Left Out.

Kings of Israel.

Captivity of Judah.

More About Jesus.

The First Volume is for Four, the last for Twelve years of age.

I.

THE PEEP OF DAY.

A SERIES OF THE EARLIEST RELIGIOUS INSTRUCTION. With Questions. 851st Thousand. 18mo. 27 Illustrations. Cloth, 2s.; roxburghe, 2s. 6d.
Cheap Edition for Schools, 18mo. limp cloth, 6d.

II.

STREAKS OF LIGHT. OR, FIFTY-TWO FACTS FROM THE BIBLE.
77th Thousand. 18mo. 52 Illustrations. Cloth, 2s. 6d.; roxburghe, 3s.

III.

LINE UPON LINE.

A SECOND SERIES OF RELIGIOUS INSTRUCTION. With Questions.
Part I. 414th Thou. 18mo. 30 Illustrations. Cloth, 2s. 6d.; roxb. 3s.
Part II. 323rd Thou. 18mo. 27 Illustrations. Cloth, 2s. 6d.; roxb. 3s.
Popular Edition, Illustrated, limp cloth, 2 parts, 9d. each.

IV.

PRECEPT UPON PRECEPT. WITH QUESTIONS.
76th Thous. 18mo. 68 Illustrations and Map. Cloth, 2s. 6d.; roxb. 3s.

V.

APOSTLES PREACHING TO JEWS AND GENTILES;
Or, THE ACTS EXPLAINED TO CHILDREN. With Questions.
32nd Thous. 18mo. 27 Illus. and Coloured Map. Cloth, 2s. 6d.; roxb. 3s.

VI.

LINES LEFT OUT. WITH QUESTIONS.
76th Thousand. 18mo. 28 Illustrations. Cloth, 2s. 6d.; roxburghe, 3s.

VII.

THE KINGS OF ISRAEL AND JUDAH.
35th Thous. 18mo. 27 Illus. and Coloured Map. Cl. 2s. 6d.; roxburghe, 3s.

VIII.

THE CAPTIVITY OF JUDAH. With Questions.
16th Thou. 18mo. 27 Illus. and Col. Map. Cloth, 2s. 6d ; roxb. 3s.

IX.

MORE ABOUT JESUS. With Questions.
67th Thousand. 18mo. 26 Illustrations. Cloth, 2s. 6d.; roxburghe, 3s

X.

READING WITHOUT TEARS.
A Pleasant Mode of Learning to Read.
Part I. 91st Thousand. Square 16mo. 520 Illus. Cloth, *large type,* 2s.6d.
Part II. 44th Thousand. Square 16mo. 130 Illus. Cloth, *large type,* 2s.6d.

(Two Parts in One Volume, cloth antique, 4s. 6d.)

XI.

READING DISENTANGLED. 21st Edition.
A Series of Classified Lessons in 37 Sheets.
4s. the set, plain ; mounted for hanging, 7s.

XII.

NEAR HOME ;
Or, Europe Described to Children.
With Anecdotes. Fifth Edition, carefully revised.
72 Illustrations, and a Map. Fcap. 8vo. cloth, 5s.

XIII.

FAR OFF. Part I. ;
Or, Asia Described. With Anecdotes.
54th Thousand. 560 pp. revised throughout. Fcap. 8vo. 5s.
With 95 small, 16 full-page, and 2 Coloured Illustrations, and Coloured Map.

XIV.

FAR OFF.   Part II. ;

    Or, OCEANIA, AFRICA, AND AMERICA DESCRIBED.   With Anecdotes.
    Embracing Recent Discoveries and other Changes.
    With above 200 Illustrations.   40th Thousand.   Crown 8vo. 5*s.*

XV.

LIGHT IN THE DWELLING;

    Or, A HARMONY OF THE FOUR GOSPELS.
    With short and simple Remarks adapted to Family Reading.
    In 365 Sections.   32nd Thousand.   Thick 8vo. cloth, 3*s.* 6*d.*

XVI.

THE NIGHT OF TOIL.

    LABOURS OF THE FIRST MISSIONARIES TO THE SOUTH-SEA ISLANDS.
    New Cheap Edition.   7th Thous.   Fcap. 8vo.   With 9 Illus.   Cloth, 3*s.*

XVII.

THE ANGEL'S MESSAGE ;

    THE SAVIOUR MADE KNOWN TO THE COTTAGER.
    27th Thousand.   Square 16mo.   9 Illustrations.   Paper cover, 2*d.*

Over 1,500,000 *Copies of Works by this Author have been sold.*

CHEAP SCHOOL EDITIONS

OF

THE PEEP OF DAY SERIES.

18mo. limp, with 340 Illustrations and 7 Maps.

1. THE PEEP OF DAY ... ... 1s. 2d.

2. STREAKS OF LIGHT ... ... 1s. 6d.

3. LINE UPON LINE. Two Parts, each... ... 1s. 4d.

4. PRECEPT UPON PRECEPT ... ... 1s. 6d.

5. APOSTLES PREACHING ... ... 1s. 4d.

6. LINES LEFT OUT ... ... 1s. 6d.

7. KINGS OF ISRAEL AND JUDAH... ... 1s. 6d.

8. THE CAPTIVITY OF JUDAH ... ... 1s. 6d.

9. MORE ABOUT JESUS ... ... 1s 4d.

LONDON, NEW YORK, & BOMBAY: LONGMANS, GREEN. & CO.

Made in United States
Orlando, FL
06 November 2022

24246786R00167